4-CHORD SONGS
FOR BARITONE UKULELE

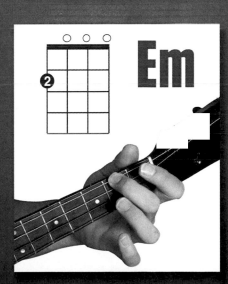

ISBN 978-1-4950-5764-9

HAL•LEONARD®
CORPORATION
7777 W. BLUEMOUND RD. P.O. BOX 13819 MILWAUKEE, WI 53213

Visit Hal Leonard Online at
www.halleonard.com

CONTENTS

Bad Blood

Words and Music by Taylor Swift, Max Martin and Shellback

Brown Eyed Girl

Words and Music by Van Morrison

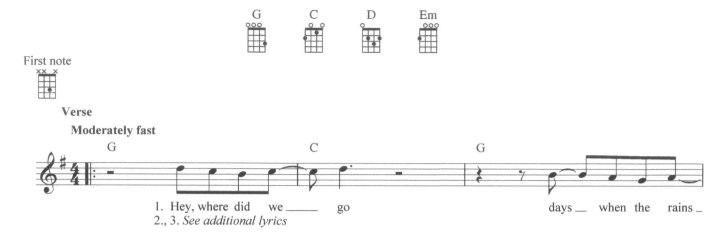

First note

Verse
Moderately fast

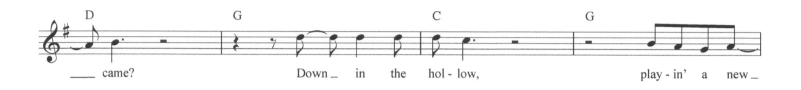

1. Hey, where did we _____ go _____ days ___ when the rains ___
2., 3. *See additional lyrics*

___ came? Down ___ in the hol - low, play - in' a new ___

___ game, laugh - ing and a - run - ning, hey, ___ hey,

skip - ping and a - jump - ing. In the mist - y morn -

- ing fog ___ with our hearts a - thump - in', and

C   D   G   Em

you,   my brown eyed girl.

You, my brown eyed girl. ____ Do you re - mem -

Chorus

- ber when we used to sing: ____ Sha la ____ la la ____

__ la la ____ la la ____ la la la te da? ____

Sha la ____ la la la ____ la la ____ la la ____ la la la te da __

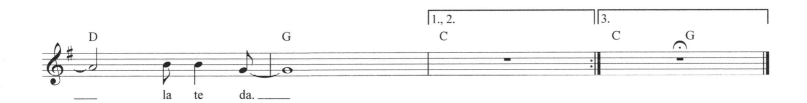

1., 2. | 3.

__ la te da. ____

Additional Lyrics

2. Whatever happened to Tuesday and so slow
   Going down the old mine with a transistor radio,
   Standing in the sunlight laughing
   Hiding behind a rainbow's wall,
   Slipping and a-sliding
   All along the waterfall
   With you, my brown eyed girl,
   You, my brown eyed girl?
   Do you remember when we used to sing:

3. So hard to find my way, now that I'm all on my own
   I saw you just the other day, my, how you have grown
   Cast my memory back there, Lord
   Sometime I'm overcome thinking 'bout
   Making love in the green grass
   Behind the stadium
   With you, my brown eyed girl,
   With you, my brown eyed girl.
   Do you remember when we used to sing:

Burn One Down

Words and Music by Ben Harper

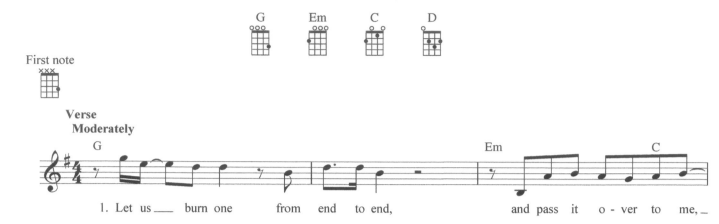

First note

Verse
Moderately

1. Let us __ burn one from end to end, and pass it o - ver to me, __

__ my friend. _____ Burn it long, __ we'll burn it slow

to light __ me up be - fore I go. If you don't like __ my fi - re, then

Chorus

don't come a - round, __ 'cause I'm gon - na burn one down. _____ Yes, I'm __

__ gon - na burn __ one _____ down. _____

Verse

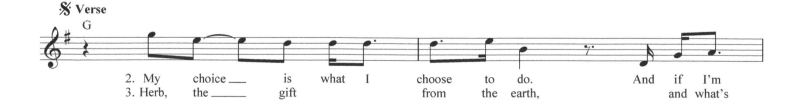

2. My choice __ is what I choose to do. And if I'm

3. Herb, the _____ gift from the earth, and what's

caus - in' no harm, ____ it should - n't both - er you. _____
from the earth ____ is of the great - est worth. _____ So be -

Your choice ____ is who you choose to be. And if you're
- fore you ____ knock it, try it first. Oh, you'll

caus - in' no harm, ____ then you're al - right with me. ____
see it's a bless - ing and it's not a curse. ____

If you

Chorus

don't like ____ my fi - re, then don't come a - round, 'cause I'm gon - na burn ____ one ____

To Coda ⊕

down. _____ Yes, I'm ____ gon - na burn ____ one down. _____

⊕ **Coda**

D.S. al Coda

____ I'm gon - na burn ____ one... ____

_____ Oh.

* Let chord ring.

9

Come On Get Higher

Words and Music by Matt Nathanson and Mark Weinberg

come on, get high - er, loos - en my lips. Faith ___ and de - sire and the swing of your hips. Just

pull me down ___ hard ___ and drown ___ me in love. ___

Bridge

I miss the pull of your ___ heart, I taste the sparks on your tongue.

I see an - gels and dev - ils and God ___ when you come ___ on, ___ hold ___

___ on, ___ hold on, ___ hold on, ___ hold on. ___

Outro-Chorus

Come on, get high - er, loos - en my lips. Faith ___ and de - sire and the swing of your hips. Just

pull me down ___ hard ___ and drown ___ me in love. ___ So

come on, get high - er, loos - en my lips. Faith ___ and de - sire and the swing of your hips. Just / Ev -

1.

pull me down ___ hard ___ and drown ___ me, drown ___ me in love.

2.

'ry - thing works, ___ love, ev - 'ry - thing works ___ in your ___ arms.

Cupid

Words and Music by Sam Cooke

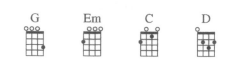

First note

Chorus
Moderately fast

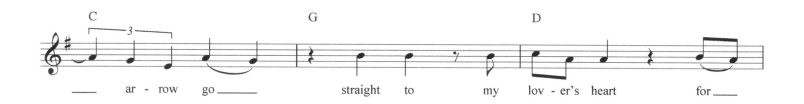

Cu - pid, draw ___ back your bow and let your ___

___ ar - row go ___ straight to my lov - er's heart for ___

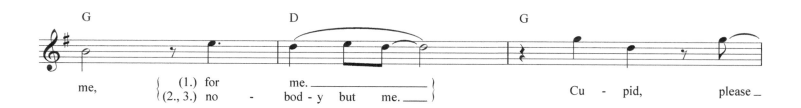

me, { (1.) for me. ___ } { (2., 3.) no - bod - y but me. ___ } Cu - pid, please ___

___ hear my cry and let your ___ ar - row fly ___

To Coda ⊕

straight to my lov - er's heart for ___ me. ___

Verse

1. Now, _____   I don't mean to both - er you, but
2. Now, _____   Cu - pid, if your ar - row'll make her

I'm in dis - tress; _____   there's dan - ger of me los - ing all of
love strong for me, _____   I prom - ise I will love her un - til

my hap - pi - ness. _____   For I love a girl who does - n't
e - ter - ni - ty. _____   I know, be - tween the two of us, her

2nd time, D.C. al Coda

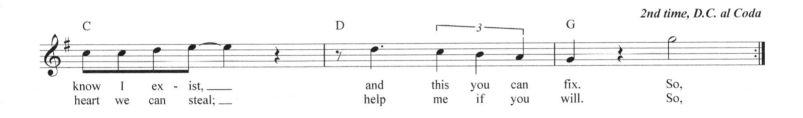

know I ex - ist, _____   and this you can fix.   So,
heart we can steal; _____   help me if you will.   So,

⊕ Coda

Outro

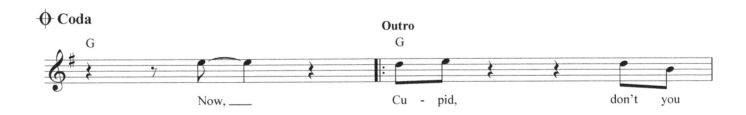

Now, _____   Cu - pid,   don't you

Repeat and fade

hear me call - ing you?   I need _____ you.

Every Rose Has Its Thorn

Words and Music by Bobby Dall, C.C. Deville, Bret Michaels and Rikki Rockett

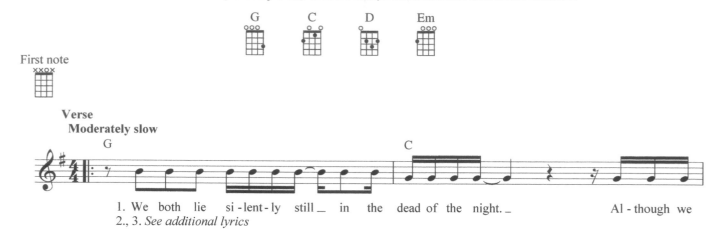

Verse
Moderately slow

1. We both lie si-lent-ly still __ in the dead of the night. __ Al-though we
2., 3. *See additional lyrics*

both lie close to-geth — er, __ we feel miles a-part __ in-side. __ Was it

some-thing I said or some-thing I did? Did my words not come out right? __ Though I

tried not to hurt __ you, __ though I tried, but I guess that's why __ they say

Chorus

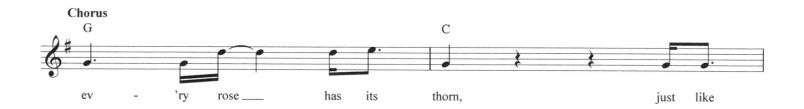

ev — 'ry rose __ has its thorn, just like

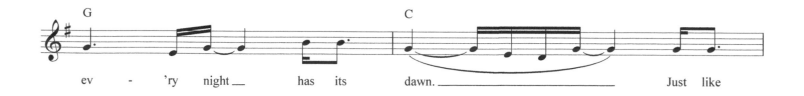

ev — 'ry night __ has its dawn. __ Just like

ev - 'ry cow - boy _____ sings his sad, sad _____ song,

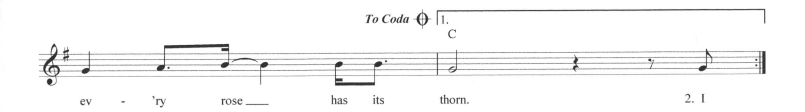

To Coda ⊕ 1.

ev - 'ry rose _____ has its thorn. 2. I

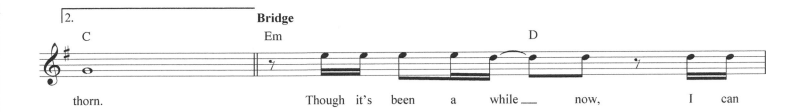

thorn. Though it's been a while ___ now, I can

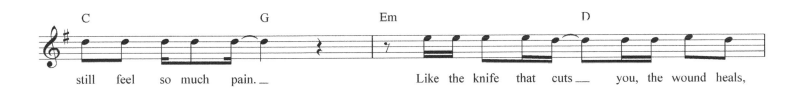

still feel so much pain. __ Like the knife that cuts ___ you, the wound heals,

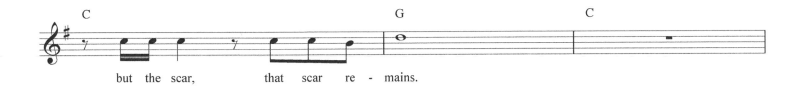

but the scar, that scar re - mains.

⊕ Coda

D.C. al Coda

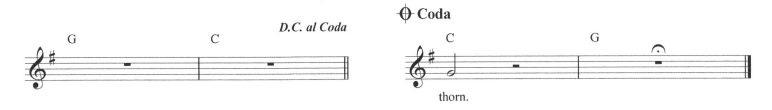

thorn.

Additional Lyrics

2. I listen to our favorite song playing on the radio,
   Hear the DJ say love's a game of easy come and easy go.
   But I wonder, does he know? Has he ever felt like this?
   And I know that you'd be here right now if I could've let you know somehow.
   I guess... *(To Chorus)*

3. I know I could have saved our love that night if I'd known what to say.
   Instead of making love, we both made our separate ways.
   And now I hear you've found somebody new and that I never meant that much to you.
   To hear that tears me up inside and to see you cuts me like a knife.
   I guess... *(To Chorus)*

Fast Car

Words and Music by Tracy Chapman

Verse

4. You got a fast ___ car, but is it fast e-nough ___ so we can fly a-way? ___

We got-ta make a de-ci-sion: ___ leave to-night ___ or live and die this way.

𝄋 **Chorus**

'Cause I re-mem-ber when we were driv-in', driv-ing in your car, ___ the

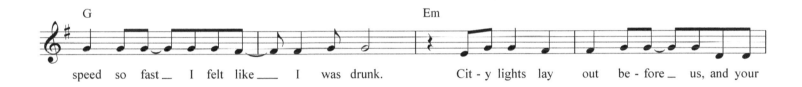

speed so fast ___ I felt like ___ I was drunk. Cit-y lights lay out be-fore ___ us, and your

arm felt nice wrapped 'round my shoul-der. And I, ___ I ___ had a

feel-ing that I ___ be-longed. ___ I, ___ I ___ had a

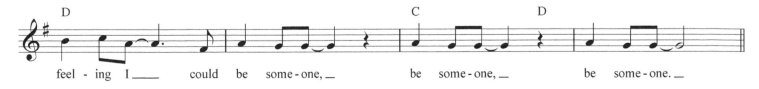

feel-ing I ___ could be some-one, ___ be some-one, ___ be some-one. ___

Interlude

Verse

5. You got a fast __ car. We go cruis - ing, en - ter - tain our - selves. __ You
6. *See additional lyrics*

still ain't got a job, _____ and I work in a mar - ket as a check - out girl. ____

I know things __ will get bet - ter; you'll find work, and I'll ____ get pro - mot - ed. __

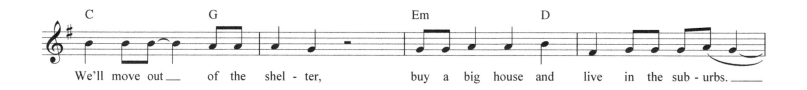

We'll move out __ of the shel - ter, buy a big house and live in the sub - urbs. ____

'Cause I re - mem - ber when we were

Coda

Verse

7. You got a fast — car, but is it fast e - nough — so you can fly a - way? —

You got - ta make a de - ci - sion: — leave to - night — or live and die this way.

Outro

Additional Lyrics

2. You got a fast car.
   I got a plan to get us out of here.
   I been working at the convenience store,
   Managed to save just a little bit of money.
   Won't have to drive too far,
   Just 'cross the border and into the city.
   You and I can both get jobs
   And finally see what it means to be living.

3. You see, my old man's got a problem.
   He live with the bottle, that's the way it is.
   He says his body's too old for working;
   I say his body's too young to look like his.
   My mama went off and left him;
   She wanted more from life than he could give.
   I said somebody's got to take care of him.
   So I quit school and that's what I did.

6. You got a fast car,
   And I got a job that pays all our bills.
   You stay out drinking late at the bar,
   See more of your friends than you do of your kids.
   I'd always hoped for better,
   Thought maybe together you and me would find it.
   I got no plans, I ain't going nowhere,
   So take your fast car and keep on driving.

Fidelity

Words and Music by Regina Spektor

Fifteen

Words and Music by Taylor Swift

them. And when you're fif - teen, feel - in' like ___ there's noth -

- in' to fig - ure out, _____ well, count to ten, ___ take it in. ___

___ This is life ___ be - fore you know who you're gon - na be. _____

Fif - teen. ___ But I did - n't know it at fif - teen.

Bridge

When all you want - ed was to be want - ed, wish you could go back ___ and

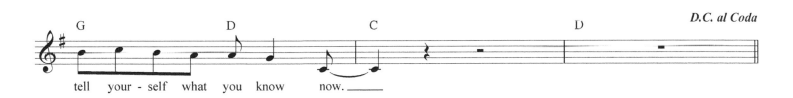

tell your - self what you know now. _____

Coda

___ And we both cried. 'Cause when you're fif - teen

and some - bod - y tells you they love ___ you, you're gon - na be - lieve ___ them. And when you're

23

fif - teen, don't _____ for - get _____ to look _____ be - fore _____ you fall. _____

_____ I've found time _____ can heal most _____ an - y - thing, _____ and you just might

find who you're sup - posed to be. _____ I did - n't know who I was s'posed to be _____

Outro

_____ at fif - teen. La la la _____ la la la _____ la la _____ la la.

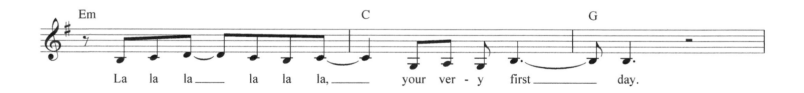

La la la _____ la la la, _____ your ver - y first _____ day. _____

Take a deep breath, girl. Take a deep breath as you walk _____ through the doors. _____

Additional Lyrics

2. You sit in class next to a redhead named Abigail,
And soon enough you're best friends,
Laughin' at the other girls who think they're so cool.
We'll be outta here as soon as we can.
And then you're on your very first date, and he's got a car,
And you're feelin' like flyin'.
And your mama's waitin' up, and you're thinkin' he's the one,
And you're dancin' 'round your room when the night ends, when the night ends.

3. Back then, I swore I was gonna marry him someday,
But I realized some bigger dreams of mine.
And Abigail gave everything she had
To a boy who changed his mind, and we both cried.

Follow You Down

Words and Music by Bill Leen, Phil Rhodes, Jesse Valenzuela, Robin Wilson and D. Scott Johnson

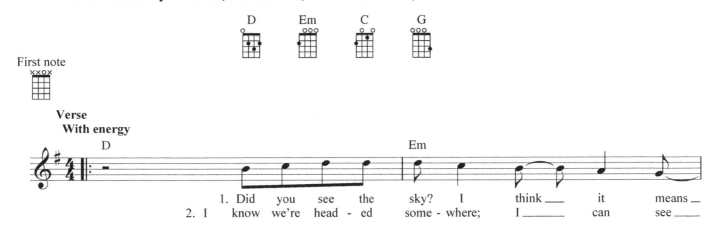

First note

Verse
With energy

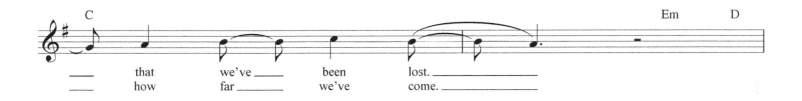

1. Did you see the sky? I think ___ it means ___
2. I know we're head-ed some-where; I ___ can see ___

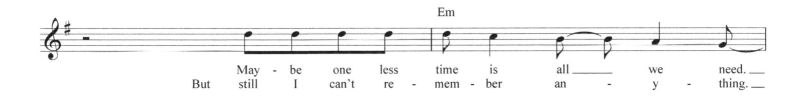

___ that we've ___ been lost. ___
___ how far ___ we've come. ___

May - be one less time is all ___ we need. ___
But still I can't re - mem - ber an - y - thing. ___

I can't real - ly
Let's not do the

help it if ___ my tongue's ___ all tied in knots. ___
wrong thing and ___ I'll swear ___ it might ___ be fun. ___

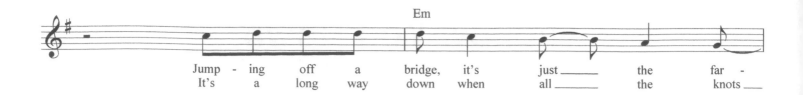

Jump - ing off a bridge, it's just _____ the far -
It's a long way down when all _____ the knots _____

- thest that _____ I've ev - er been. _____
_____ we've tied _____ have come _____ un - done. _____

𝄋 **Chorus**

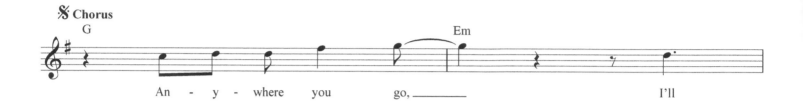

An - y - where you go, _____ I'll

fol - low _____ you down, _____ an - y - place but those _____

_____ I know _____ by heart. _____

An - y - where you go, _____ I'll fol - low _____ you down. _____

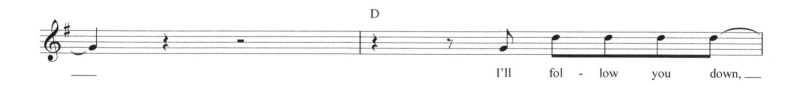

_____ I'll fol - low you down, _____

To Coda ⊕

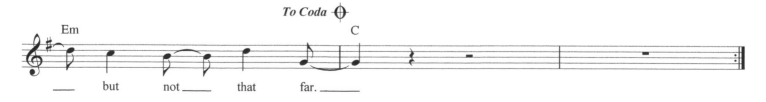

_____ but not _____ that far. _____

Bridge

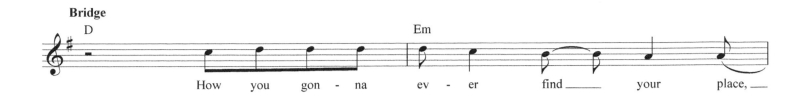

How you gon - na ev - er find your place,

run - ning an

ar - ti - fi - cial pace?

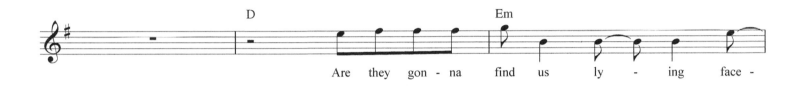

Are they gon - na find us ly - ing face -

- down in the sand? So, what the hell,

D.S al Coda

now we've al - read - y been for - ev - er damned.

Coda **Outro**

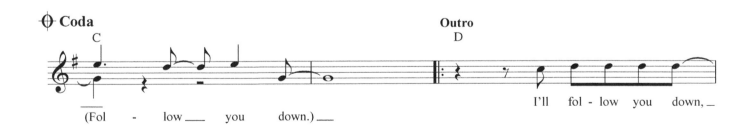

(Fol - low you down.) I'll fol - low you down,

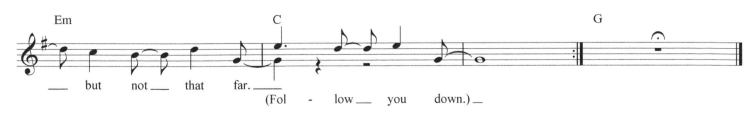

but not that far. (Fol - low you down.)

Garden Party

Words and Music by Rick Nelson

First note

§ Verse

Moderately slow, in 2

1. I went to a gar-den par-ty, to rem-i-
2.–4. *See additional lyrics*

nisce with my ___ old friends; ___ a chance to share ___ old mem-

-o-ries ___ and play our songs a-gain. When I

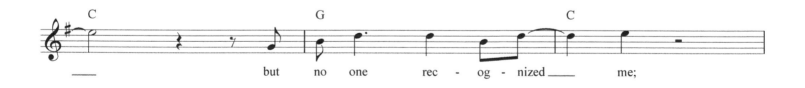

got to the gar-den par-ty, they all knew my name, ___

___ but no one rec-og-nized ___ me;

I did-n't look the same. ___ But it's **Chorus** all right now, ___

I learned my les - son well. ____ You see, you

can't please ev - 'ry - one, ____ so you got to please your - self. ____

To Coda ⊕

1.   2., 3.   **Interlude**

La da da, ____

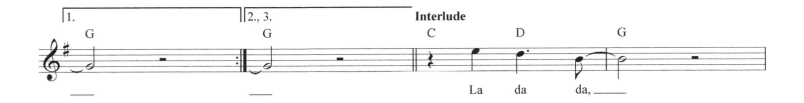

la da da da da. ____

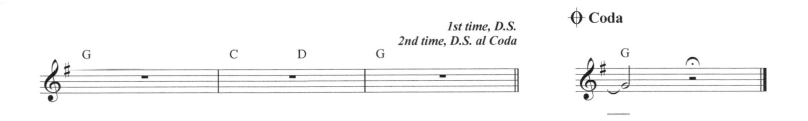

1st time, D.S.
2nd time, D.S. al Coda

⊕ **Coda**

Additional Lyrics

2. People came for miles around; everyone was there.
   Yoko brought her walrus; there was magic in the air.
   And over in the corner, much to my surprise,
   Mr. Hughes hid in Dylan's shoes, wearing his disguise.

3. I played them all the old songs; I thought that's why they came.
   No one heard the music; we didn't look the same.
   I said hello to Mary Lou; she belongs to me.
   When I sang a song about a honky-tonk, it was time to leave.

4. Someone opened up a closet door and out stepped Johnny B. Goode,
   Playing guitar like a-ringin' a bell, and lookin' like he should.
   If you gotta play at garden parties, I wish you a lotta luck;
   But if memories were all I sang, I'd rather drive a truck.

Girls Just Want to Have Fun

Words and Music by Robert Hazard

When the work - ing day ___ is done, ___ oh, girls, ___ they wan - na have fu -

un. Oh, ___ girls ___ just wan - na have ___ fun. _____

To Coda ⊕

D.C. al Coda
(take 2nd ending)

⊕ **Coda**

Outro

They just wan - na, they just wan - na. ___

They just wan - na, they just wan - na. ___ Girls, ___

Repeat and fade

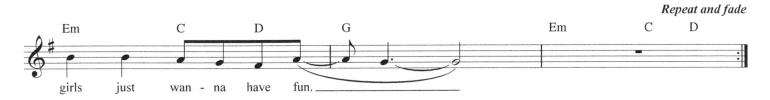

girls just wan - na have fun. _____

Additional Lyrics

2. The phone rings in the middle of the night.
   My father yells, "What you gonna do with your life?"
   Oh, Daddy dear, you know you're still number one.
   But girls, they wanna have fun.
   Oh, girls just wanna have... *(To Bridge)*

3. Some boys take a beautiful girl
   And hide her away from the rest of the world.
   I wanna be the one to walk in the sun.
   Oh, girls, they wanna have fun.
   Oh, girls just wanna have... *(To Bridge)*

Good Riddance
(Time of Your Life)

Words by Billie Joe
Music by Green Day

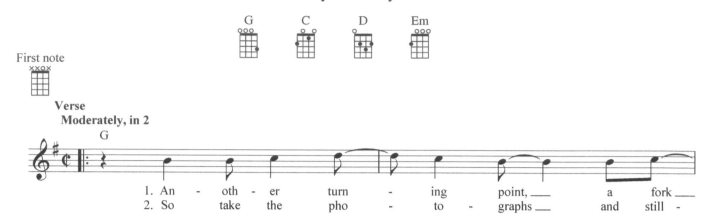

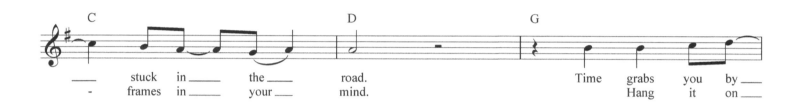

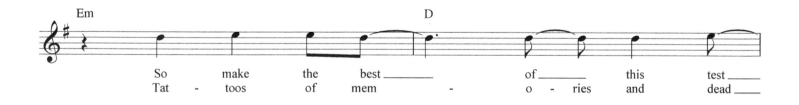

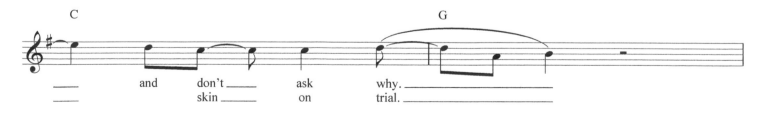

Em   D

It's   not   a   ques - tion,   but _____   a   les -
For   what   it's   worth, _____   it _____   was   worth

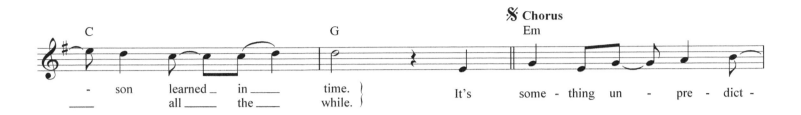

                                             𝄉 Chorus
C   G   Em

- son   learned __ in ___ time. ⎫
___   all ___ the ___ while. ⎭   It's   some - thing   un - pre - dict -

G   Em   G

- a - ble, ___   but   in   the   end ___   it's   right. ___   I

                                                        To Coda ⊕
Em   D

hope   you   had ___   the   time _____   of _____   your   life. ___

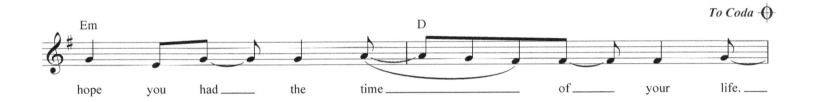

G   C

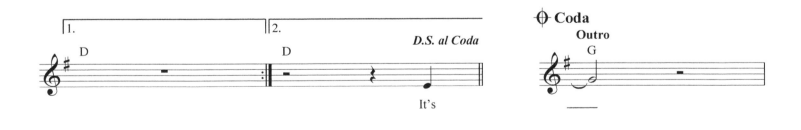

⎹1.   ⎹2.   ⊕ Coda
                                             Outro
                          D.S. al Coda
D   D   G

It's

            C   D   G

33

Have a Cigar

Words and Music by Roger Waters

First note

Verse
Moderate Rock

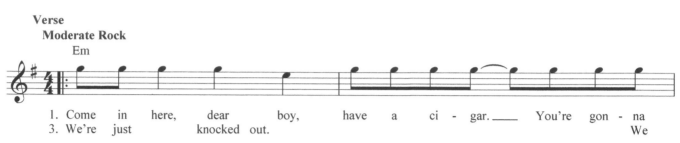

1. Come in here, dear boy, have a ci - gar.___ You're gon - na
3. We're just knocked out. We

go far.
heard a - bout the sell - out. You're gon - na fly high. You're
You got - ta get an al - bum out; you

nev - er gon - na die. You're gon - na make___ it if___ you try. They're___ gon - na
owe it to___ the peo - ple. We're so hap - py we can hard - ly count.___

love you.
2. Well, I've

Verse

Em

al - ways had a deep re - spect, and I mean that most sin - cere - ly.
4. Ev-'ry-bod-y else is just green. Have ___ you see the chart?

C

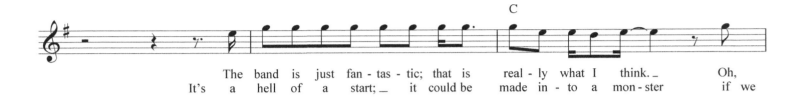

The band is just fan - tas - tic; that is real - ly what I think. ___ Oh,
It's a hell of a start; ___ it could be made in - to a mon - ster if we

D   Em

by the way, which one's Pink?
all pull to - geth - er as a team.

Chorus

C   D   Em   C

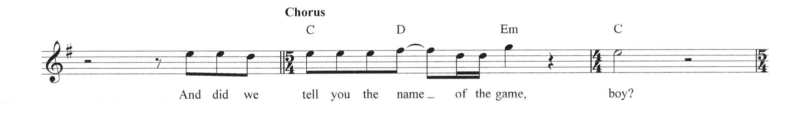

And did we tell you the name ___ of the game, boy?

D   G

We call it "Rid - ing the Gra - vy Train." _____

C   G   N.C.   Em

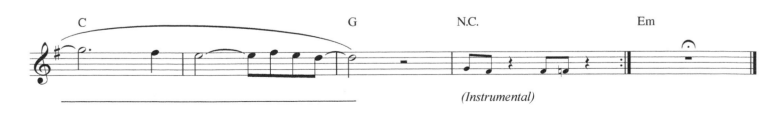

_____   *(Instrumental)*

Have You Ever Seen the Rain?

Words and Music by John Fogerty

Hey, Soul Sister

Words and Music by Pat Monahan, Espen Lind and Amund Bjorklund

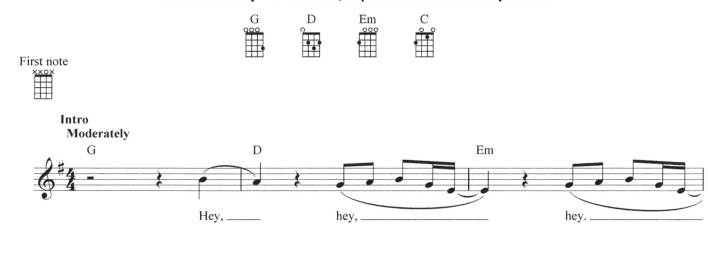

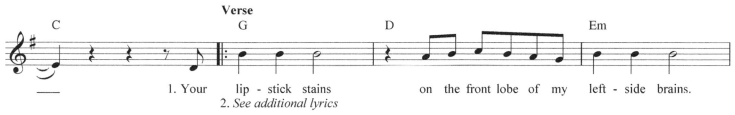

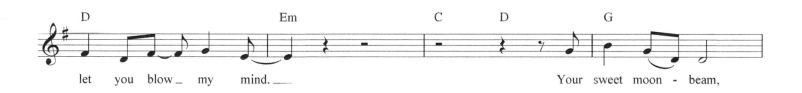

cid - ed who's one of my kind. ____

Hey, soul sis - ter, ain't ____ that Mis - ter Mis - ter on the ra - di - o, ____ ster - e - o? ____ The way ____

To Coda ⊕

____ you move ____ ain't fair, you know. ____ Hey, soul sis - ter, I ____ don't wan - na miss a sin - gle

1.

thing you do ____ to - night. ____ Hey, ____ hey, ____

2.
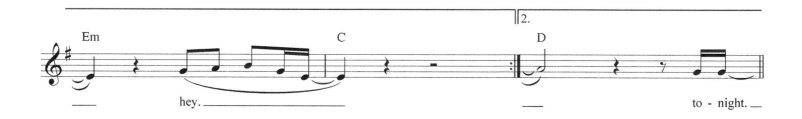

____ hey. ____ ____ to - night. ____

Bridge
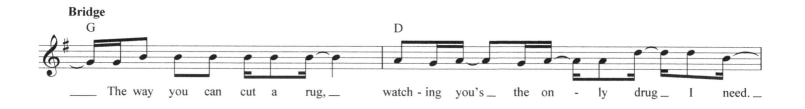

____ The way you can cut a rug, ____ watch - ing you's ____ the on - ly drug ____ I need. ____

____ Some gang - sta, I'm ____ so thug. ____ You're the on - ly one ____ I'm dream - in' of. ____ You see,

I can be my-self now, fi-nal-ly. In fact,— there's noth-in' I— can't be.—

D.S. al Coda

— I want the world to see— you'll be— with— me.

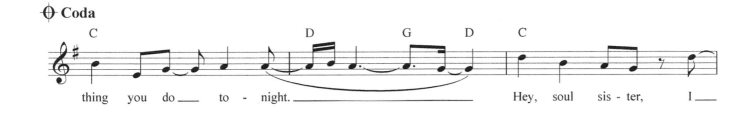

Coda

thing you do— to - night. ——— Hey, soul sis - ter, I—

— don't wan - na miss a sin - gle thing you do ——— to - night. —

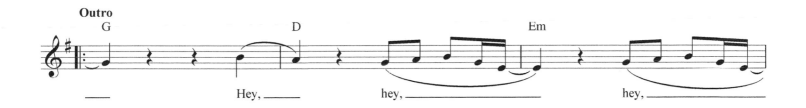

Outro

— Hey, ——— hey, ——— hey, ———

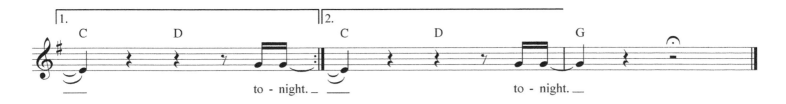

1.
— to - night. —

2.
to - night. —

Additional Lyrics

2. Just in time, I'm so glad you have a one-track mind like me.
You gave my life direction,
A game-show love connection we can't deny.
I'm so obsessed, my heart is bound to beat right out my un-trimmed chest.
I believe in you. Like a virgin, you're Madonna
And I'm always gonna wanna blow your mind.

Home

Words and Music by Jade Castrinos and Alex Ebert

Hush-a-bye

Words by Mort Shuman
Music by Doc Pomus

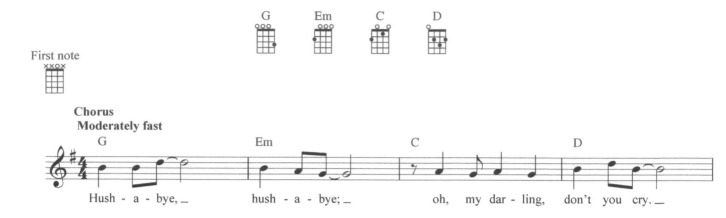

Chorus
Moderately fast

Hush - a - bye, hush - a - bye; oh, my dar - ling, don't you cry.

Guard - ian an - gels up a - bove, take care of the one I love.

Interlude

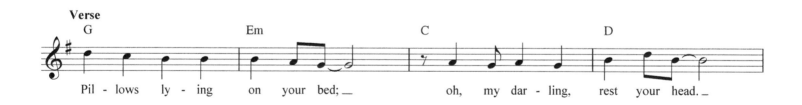

Ooh, ooh.

Verse

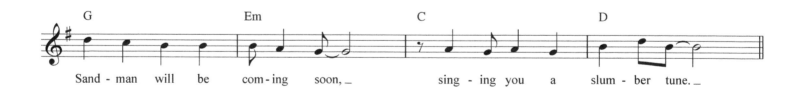

Pil - lows ly - ing on your bed; oh, my dar - ling, rest your head.

Sand - man will be com - ing soon, sing - ing you a slum - ber tune.

Interlude

Ooh, ooh.

Ooh. _____ Lull - a -

Bridge

by _____ and good - night, _____ in your

dreams _____ I'll hold you tight. _____ Lull - a -

by _____ and good - night, _____ till the

dawn's _____ ear - ly light. _____

Chorus

Hush - a - bye, _ hush - a - bye; _ oh, my dar - ling, don't you cry. _

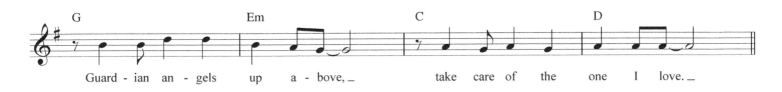

Guard - ian an - gels up a - bove, _ take care of the one I love. _

Outro   *Repeat and fade*

Ooh, _____ ooh. _____

I Knew You Were Trouble

Words and Music by Taylor Swift, Shellback and Max Martin

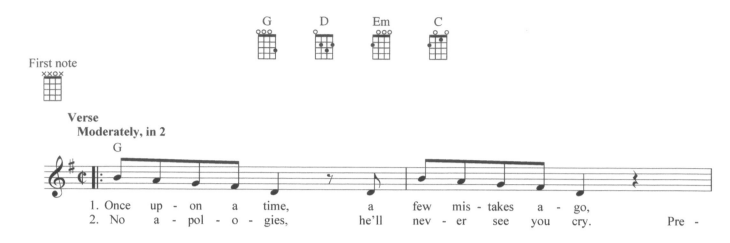

First note

Verse
Moderately, in 2

1. Once up - on a time, a few mis - takes a - go,
2. No a - pol - o - gies, he'll nev - er see you cry. Pre -

I was in your sights, you got me a - lone. You found ____ me, you
tends he does - n't know that he's the rea - son why you're drown - ing, you're

found ____ me, you found ____ me, ee, ee, ee, ee. I
drown - ing, you're drown - ing, ing, ing, ing, ing. And I

guess you did - n't care, and I guess I liked that. And when I fell hard, you
heard you moved _ on, from whis - pers on the street. A new notch in your belt is

took a step back with - out ____ me, with - out ____ me, with -
all I'll ev - er be. And now ____ I see, now ____ I see,

Pre-Chorus

out ____ me, ee, ee, ee, ee. ____ And he's long ____
now ____ I see, ee, ee, ee, ee. ____ He was long ____

gone   when he's   next _____ to _____
gone   when he   met _____

me,   and I   re   -   a - lize _____   the blame   is   on _____
me,   and I   re   -   a - lize _____   the joke   is   on _____

𝄉 Chorus

me. ___   'Cause   I   knew   you   were   trou - ble   when you walked   in, _____
me. ___

___   so   shame   on   me   now. _____   Flew   me   to

plac - es   I'd   nev - er   been _____   till   you   put   me   down.   Oh,

I   knew   you   were   trou - ble   when   you   walked   in, _____   so

shame   on   me   now. _____   Flew   me   to   plac - es   I'd   nev - er   been.

Now I'm ly - ing on the cold, hard ground. Oh,

oh, trou - ble, trou - ble, trou - ble.

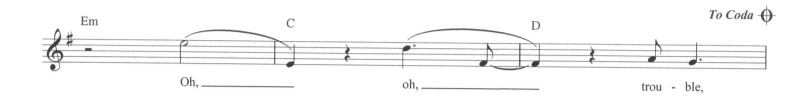

Oh, oh, trou - ble,

1. trou - ble, trou - ble. 2. trou - ble, trou - ble. And the sad - dest fear comes

creep - ing in, that you nev - er loved me or her, or

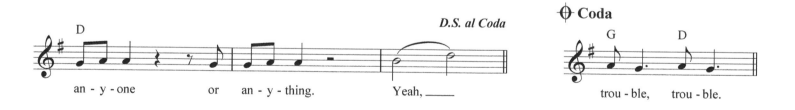

an - y - one or an - y - thing. Yeah, trou - ble, trou - ble.

I knew you were trou - ble when you walked in. Trou - ble, trou - ble, trou - ble.

I knew you were trou - ble when you walked in. Trou - ble, trou - ble, trou - ble.

How to Save a Life

Words and Music by Joseph King and Isaac Slade

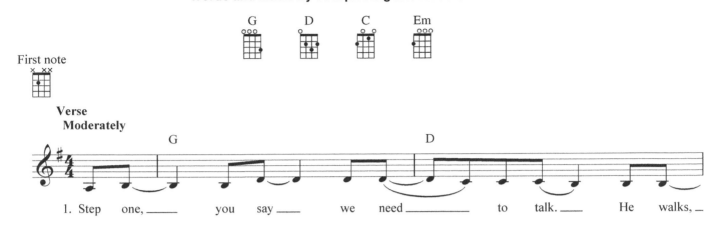

Verse
Moderately

1. Step one, ____ you say ____ we need ____ to talk. ____ He walks, ___

____ you say, ___ "Sit down, ___ it's just ___ a talk." He smiles po - lite -

- ly back at you. You stare po - lite - ly right on through

some sort of win - dow to ____ your right, as he ____ goes left ___

____ and you ___ stay ___ right. ____ Be - tween ___ the lines ___ of fear and blame,

you be - gin to won - der why ____ you came.

Chorus

Where did I _____ go wrong? _____ } I lost _____ a friend
where did I _____ go wrong? _____ }

some - where _ a - long _____ in the bit - ter - ness. And I would have _ stayed _ up _

_____ with you _ all night had I _____ known how to save _____ a life. _

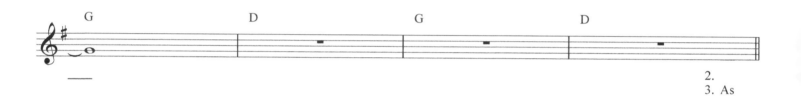

_____

2.
3. As

Verse

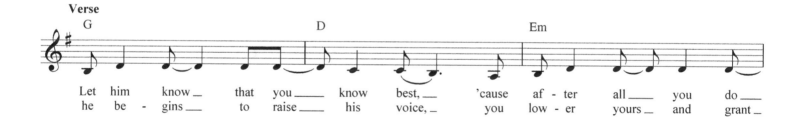

Let him know _ that you _____ know best, _ 'cause af - ter all _____ you do _____
he be - gins _____ to raise _____ his voice, _ you low - er yours _ and grant _

_____ know best. _____ Try to slip past his _____ de - fense _____
_____ him one _____ last choice. _ Drive un - til you lose _____ the road _____ or

with - out grant - ing in - no - cence. _____ Lay down _ a list _____
break with the ones you've fol - lowed. _____ He will _____ do one _

48

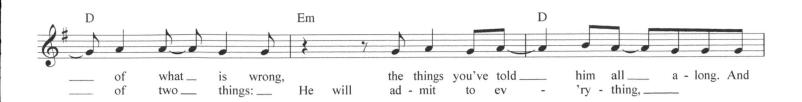

D   Em   D

_____ of what _ is wrong,   the things you've told _____ him all _____ a - long. And
_____ of two _ things: _ He will ad - mit to ev - 'ry - thing, _____

G   D

pray to God _____ he hears _____ you,   and
or he'll say _____ he's just not the same   and

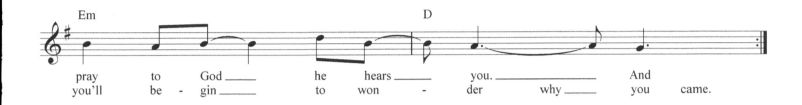

Em   D

pray to God _____ he hears _____ you. _____ And
you'll be - gin _____ to won - der why _____ you came.

Chorus

C   D   Em

Where did I _____ go wrong? _ I lost _____ a friend some - where _ a - long _

G   D   C   D

_____ in the bit - ter - ness. And I would have _ stayed _ up _____ with you _ all night

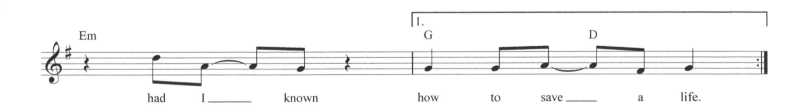

1.

Em   G   D

had I _____ known how to save _____ a life.

2.

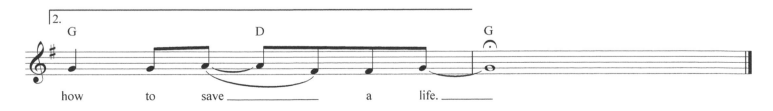

G   D   G

how to save _____ a life. _____

I'll Be

Words and Music by Edwin McCain

stead of the gal - lows of heart - ache that hang from a - bove.

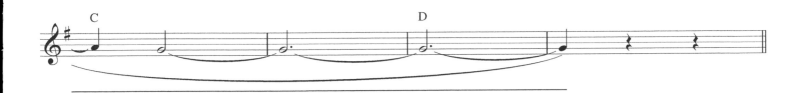

𝄋 Chorus

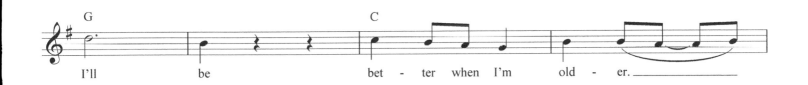

I'll be your cry - in' shoul - der.

I'll be love su - i - cide. And

I'll be bet - ter when I'm old - er.

To Coda ⊕

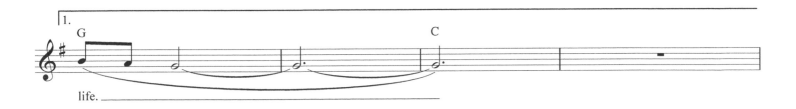

I'll be the great - est fan of your

1.

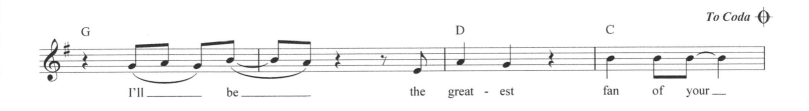

life.

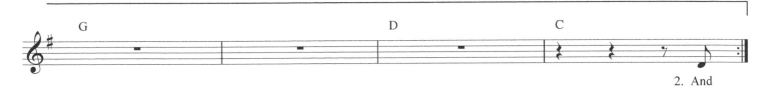

2. And

51

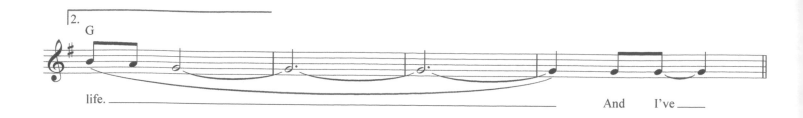

2. G

life. _____ And I've ___

Bridge

Em   D

dropped out, I've burned up, I've fought my way back from the dead. _

C

_____ I've

Em   D

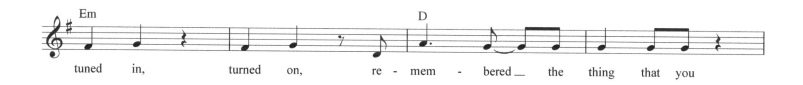

tuned in, turned on, re - mem - bered _ the thing that you

C   D   *D.S. al Coda*

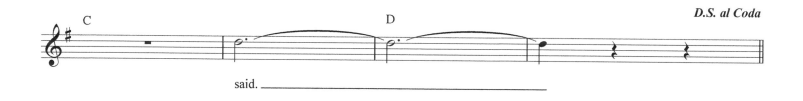

said. _____

⊕ Coda
Outro

G   C

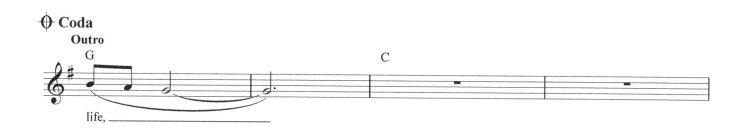

life, _____

G   D   C   G

the great - est _ fan of your _ life.

If I Had a Hammer
(The Hammer Song)

Words and Music by Lee Hays and Pete Seeger

Additional Lyrics

2. If I had a bell, I'd ring it in the morning,
   I'd ring it in the evening all over this land.
   I'd ring out danger, I'd ring out a warning,
   I'd ring out love between my brothers and my sisters,
   All over this land.

3. If I had a song, I'd sing it in the morning,
   I'd sing it in the evening all over this land.
   I'd sing out danger, I'd sing out a warning,
   I'd sing out love between my brothers and my sisters,
   All over this land.

4. Well, I got a hammer, and I've got a bell,
   And I've got a song to sing all over this land.
   It's the hammer of justice, it's the bell of freedom,
   It's the song about love between my brothers and my sisters,
   All over this land.

Last Kiss

Words and Music by Wayne Cochran

First note

Intro-Chorus
Moderately fast

Well, where, oh, where can my ___ ba - by be? The Lord took her a -

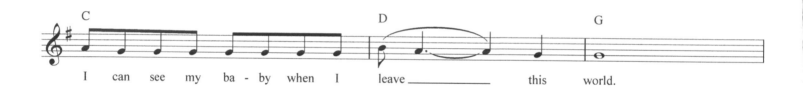

way from me. ___ She's gone to heav - en, so I got to be good ___ so

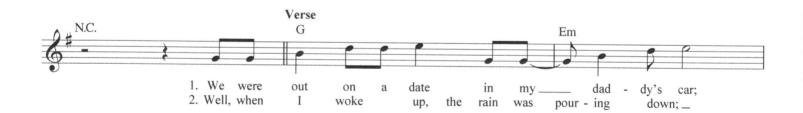

I can see my ba - by when I leave _____ this world.

Verse

1. We were out on a date in my ___ dad - dy's car;
2. Well, when I woke up, the rain was pour - ing down; ___

we had - n't driv - en ver - y far. ___ There in the road ___
there were peo - ple stand - in' all a - round. ___ Some - thing warm ___ a - run - nin'

straight a - head, ___ a car was stalled; the en - gine was dead. ___
in my eyes, ___ but I found ___ my ba - by some - how that night. ___ I

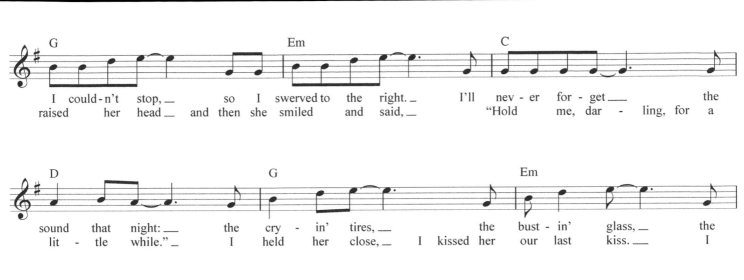

I could-n't stop, _ so I swerved to the right. _ I'll nev - er for - get _ the
raised her head _ and then she smiled and said, _ "Hold me, dar - ling, for a

sound that night: _ the cry - in' tires, _ the bust - in' glass, _ the
lit - tle while." _ I held her close, _ I kissed her our last kiss. _ I

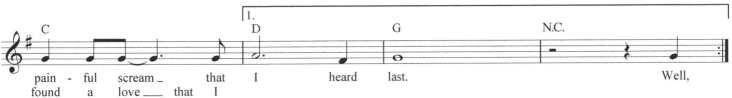

1.

pain - ful scream _ that I heard last. Well,
found a love _ that I

2.

knew I would miss. _ But now she's gone; _ e - ven though I hold her tight, I

lost my love, _ my life that night. Well,

Outro-Chorus

where, oh, where can my _ ba - by be? The Lord took her a -

way from me. _ She's gone to heav - en, so I got to be good _ so

I can see my ba - by when I leave _ this world.

Learning to Fly

Words and Music by Tom Petty and Jeff Lynne

Let It Be

Words and Music by John Lennon and Paul McCartney

Little Lies

Words and Music by Dave Barnes

la, these lit-tle lies. _____ There's a dev - il on my shoul-der, ba -

by, ooh, _____ and I be - lieve ___

___ too man - y things he says; ___ yeah, _____ yeah, yeah. ___

I'm fight-ing these fears as I find the truth, _____ and I'm

Interlude

sor - ry for hurt - ing you. *(Instrumental)*

Outro-Chorus

La la la la la la la, these lit - tle lies. La la la la la la

la, these lit - tle lies. ___ La la la la la la la, these lit - tle lies.

La la la la la la la, these lit - tle lies. la, these lit - tle lies.

Lookin' Out My Back Door

Words and Music by John Fogerty

First note

Verse
Moderately, in 2

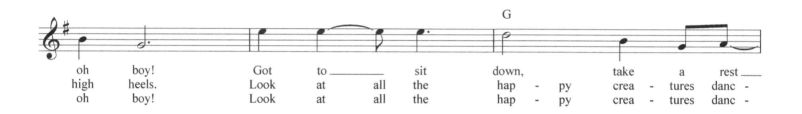

1. Just got home from Il - li - nois, __ lock the front __ door,
(2.) gi - ant do - ing cart - wheels, a stat - ue wear - in'
3. For - ward trou - bles Il - li - nois, __ lock the front __ door,

oh boy! Got to __ sit down, take a rest __
high heels. Look at all the hap - py crea - tures danc -
oh boy! Look at all the hap - py crea - tures danc -

__ on the porch. __ I - mag - i - na - tion
- ing on the lawn. __ A di - no - saur __ Vic -
- ing on the lawn. __ Both - er me __ to -

sets in, pret - ty soon __ I'm sing - in',
tro - la lis - t'ning to __ Buck O - wens. ⎫
mor - row, to - day I'll buy __ no sor - rows. ⎭

Chorus

To Coda ⊕ | 1.

Doo, doo, doo, look - in' out my back door. 2. There's a

door.   Tam - bou - rines ___   and   el - e - phants   are

play - ing   in   the   band. ___   Won't   you   take   a   ride ___

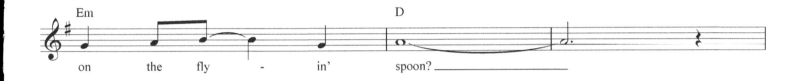

on   the   fly - in'   spoon? ___

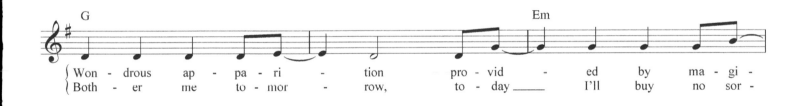

Won - drous   ap - pa - ri - tion   pro - vid - ed   by   ma - gi -
Both - er   me   to - mor - row,   to - day ___   I'll   buy   no   sor -

- cian.   Doo,   doo,   doo,   look - in'   out ___
- rows.

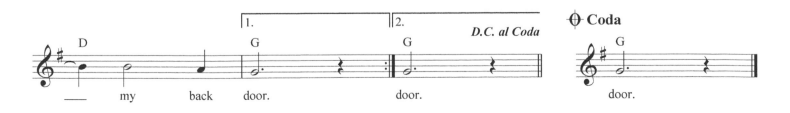

___ my   back   door.   door.   door.

Love Stinks

Words and Music by Peter Wolf and Seth Justman

Interlude

Shoo de bop.   Shoo de bop.   Shoo de bop.   Shoo, shoo.

Bridge

I've been through dia-monds   and I've been through minks.   I've

Chorus

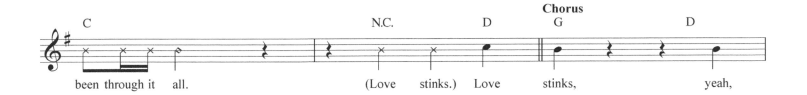

been through it all.   (Love stinks.) Love   stinks,   yeah,

yeah. __ (Love stinks.) Love   stinks,   yeah,   yeah. __

Interlude

Love

Outro-Chorus

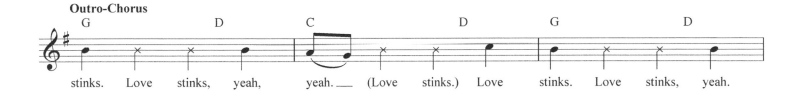

stinks. Love   stinks, yeah,   yeah. __ (Love   stinks.) Love   stinks. Love   stinks, yeah.

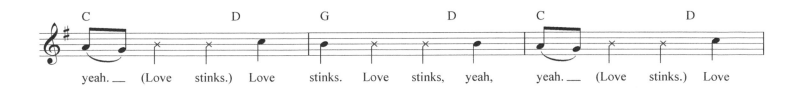

yeah. __ (Love stinks.) Love   stinks. Love   stinks, yeah,   yeah. __ (Love   stinks.) Love

stinks. I mean, it   stinks. _ Yeah,   yeah. __ (Love   stinks.) Love   stinks.

Mine

Words and Music by Taylor Swift

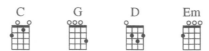

First note

Verse
Moderately fast

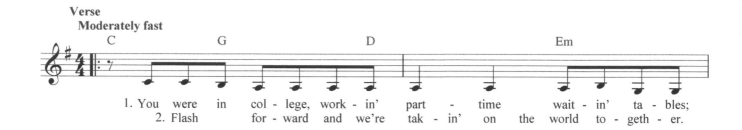

1. You were in col - lege, work - in' part - time wait - in' ta - bles;
2. Flash for - ward and we're tak - in' on the world to - geth - er.

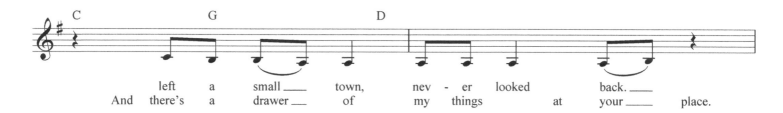

left a small ___ town, nev - er looked back. ___
And there's a drawer ___ of my things at your ___ place.

I was a flight ___ risk with a fear of fall - in',
You learn my se - crets and you fig - ure out why I'm guard - ed.

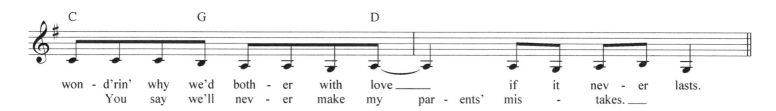

won - d'rin' why we'd both - er with love ___ if it nev - er lasts.
You say we'll nev - er make my par - ents' mis - takes. ___

Pre-Chorus

I say, ___ "Can you be - lieve ___ it?" ___
But we got bills to pay; ___

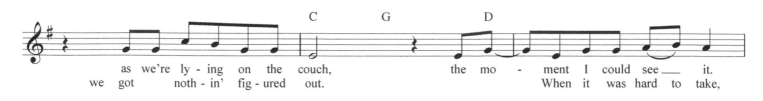

as we're ly - ing on the couch, the mo - ment I could see ___ it.
we got noth - in' fig - ured out. When it was hard to take,

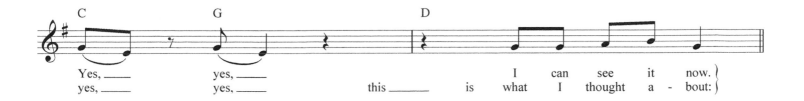

Yes, _____ yes, _____ I can see it now.
yes, _____ yes, _____ this _____ is what I thought a - bout:

Chorus

Do you re - mem - ber? We were sit - tin' there by the wa - ter.

You put your arm a - round me _____ for the first time.

You made a reb - el of a care - less man's care - ful daugh - ter.

1.

You are the best thing that's ev - er been mine. _____

2.   **Chorus**

that's ev - er been mine. Do you re - mem - ber all the cit - y lights on the wa - ter?

You saw me start to be - lieve _____ for the first time. You made a reb - el of a

care - less man's care - ful daugh - ter. You are the best thing that's ev - er been mine.

Oh, oh, oh. And I re -

Bridge

mem - ber that fight, two - thir - ty A. M., 'cause ev - 'ry - thing was slip - pin' right

out of our hands. I ran out cry - in' and you

fol - lowed me out in - to the street.

Braced my - self for the good - bye, 'cause that's all

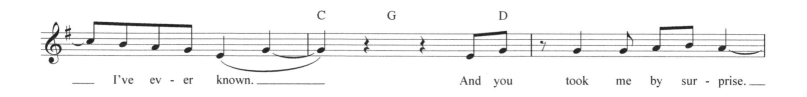

I've ev - er known. And you took me by sur - prise.

You said, "I'll nev - er leave you a - lone."

Chorus

You said, "I re-mem-ber how we felt sit-tin' by the wa-ter.

And ev-'ry time I look at you,___ it's like the first time. I fell in love with a

care-less man's care-ful daugh-ter. She is the best___ thing that's ev-er been___ mine."___

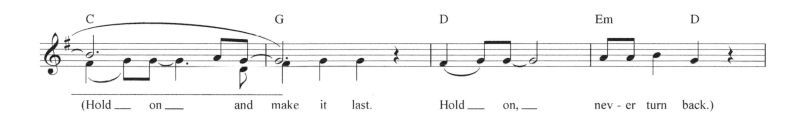

(Hold___ on___ and make it last. Hold___ on,___ nev-er turn back.)

You made a reb-el of a care-less's man's care-ful daugh-ter.

Outro

You are the best thing that's ev-er been mine.___
(Hold___ on.)___

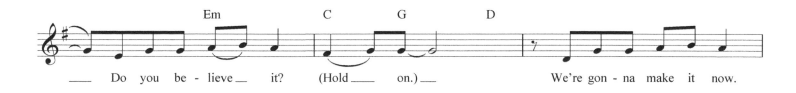

___ Do you be-lieve___ it? (Hold___ on.)___ We're gon-na make it now.

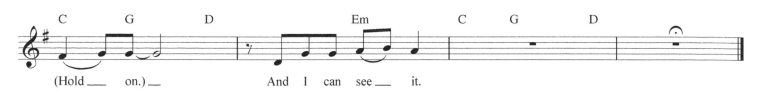

(Hold___ on.)___ And I can see___ it.

On the Turning Away

Words and Music by David Jon Gilmour and Anthony John Moore

Additional Lyrics

3. On the wings of the night,
As the daytime is stirring,
Where the speechless unite in a silent accord,
Using words you will find are strange,
Mesmerized as they light the flame.
Feel the new wind of change on the wings of the night.

4. No more turning away
From the weak and the weary.
No more turning away from the coldness inside.
Just a world that we all must share.
It's not enough just to stand and stare.
Is it only a dream that there'll be no more turning away?

Let Her Cry

Words and Music by Darius Carlos Rucker, Everett Dean Felber, Mark William Bryan and James George Sonefeld

First note

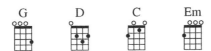

Verse
Moderately slow Rock

1. She sits a - lone by a lamp - post _____

tryin' to find a thought that's es - caped __ her mind. _____

She says, "Dad's __ the one I _____ love _____ the most, _____

but Stipe's __ not far be - hind." _____

Verse

2. She nev - er lets me in, ___ on - ly tells ___ me where she's ___ been ___
3., 4. *See additional lyrics*

when she's had ___ too much to drink. ___

I say that I don't ___ care. ___ I just run my hands through her dark hair, ___ then I

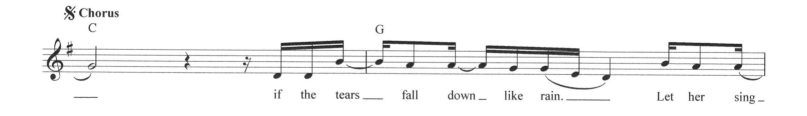

pray to God, ___ "You got - ta help me fly ___ a - way." ___ And just let her cry ___

𝄋 Chorus

___ if the tears ___ fall down ___ like rain. ___ Let her sing ___

___ if it eas - es all ___ her pain. ___ Let her go, ___

let her walk ___ right out on ___ me. _____ And if the

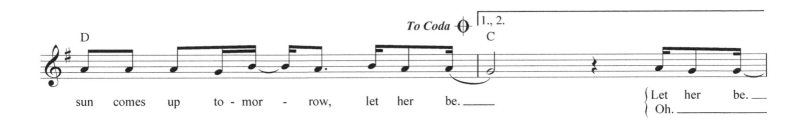

sun comes up to - mor - row, let her be. _____ Let her be. ___ / Oh. _____

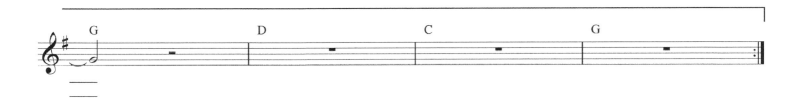

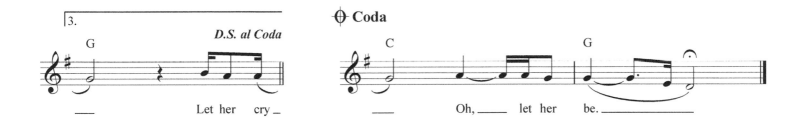

3.

D.S. al Coda

___ Let her cry ___

Coda

___ Oh, ___ let her be. _____

Additional Lyrics

3. This morning I woke up alone,
   Found a note standing by the phone
   Sayin', "Maybe, maybe I'll be back someday."
   I wanted to look for you; you walked in.
   I didn't know just what to do,
   So I sat back down, had a beer and felt sorry for myself.

4. Last night I tried to leave.
   Cried so much, I could not believe
   She was the same girl I fell in love with long ago.
   She went in the back to get high.
   I sat down on my couch and cried,
   Yelling, "Oh, Mama, please help me. Won't you hold my hand?"

One Love

Words and Music by Bob Marley

First note

Chorus
Relaxed Reggae beat

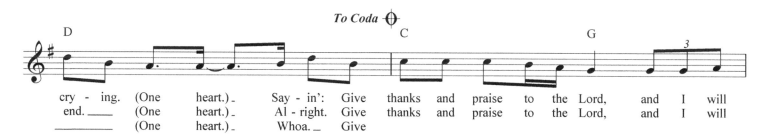

One love, __ one heart. __ Let's get to-geth-er and

feel all right. Hear the chil-dren cry - ing. (One love.) __ Hear the chil-dren
As it was in the be - gin-ning, (One love.) __ so shall it be in the
I'm plead-ing to __ man - kind. (One love.) __ Oh, Lord. _____

To Coda ⊕

cry - ing. (One heart.) __ Say - in': Give thanks and praise to the Lord, and I will
end. ____ (One heart.) __ Al - right. Give thanks and praise to the Lord, and I will
_____ (One heart.) __ Whoa. __ Give

feel all right. Say - in': Let's get to - geth - er and
feel all right. Say - in': Let's get to - geth - er and

Verse

feel all right. Whoa, whoa, whoa, whoa. 1. Let them all pass all __ their
feel all right. One more thing. 2. Let's get to - geth - er __ to

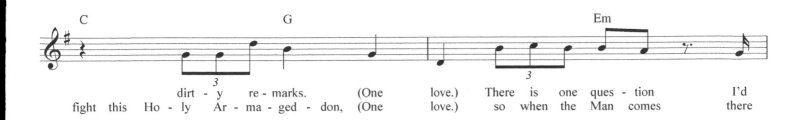

dirt - y re - marks. (One love.) There is one ques - tion I'd
fight this Ho - ly Ar - ma - ged - don, (One love.) so when the Man comes there

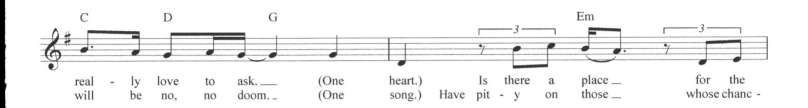

real - ly love to ask. __ (One heart.) Is there a place __ for the
will be no, no doom. _ (One song.) Have pit - y on those __ whose chanc -

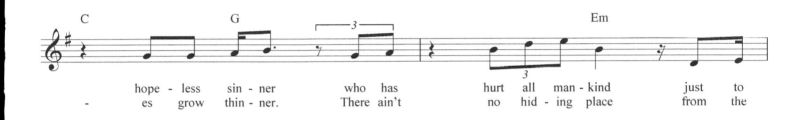

hope - less sin - ner who has hurt all man - kind just to
- es grow thin - ner. There ain't no hid - ing place from the

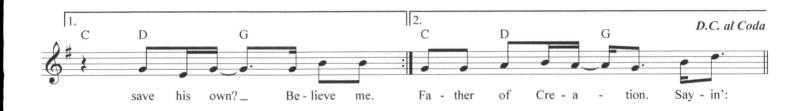

save his own? _ Be - lieve me. Fa - ther of Cre - a - tion. Say - in':

Coda

thanks and praise to the Lord, and I will feel all right.

Let's get to - geth - er and feel all right. Give feel all right.

One of Us

Words and Music by Eric Bazilian

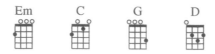

First note

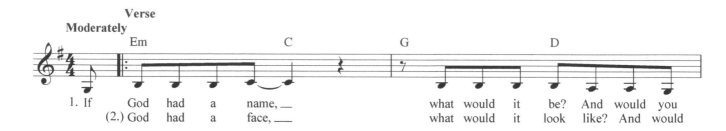

1. If God had a name, ___ what would it be? And would you
(2.) God had a face, ___ what would it look like? And would

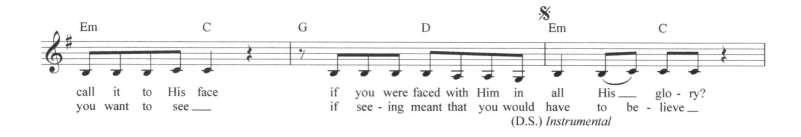

call it to His face if you were faced with Him in all His ___ glo - ry?
you want to see ___ if see - ing meant that you would have to be - lieve ___
(D.S.) *Instrumental*

What would you ask if you had just one ques - tion?
in things like heav - en and in Je - sus and the saints and all the proph - ets?
End instrumental

Pre-Chorus

Yeah, yeah, God is ___ great. Yeah, yeah, God is ___ good. Yeah, yeah,

Chorus

yeah, yeah, yeah. What if God was one of us, just a slob like one of us,

just a stran - ger on the bus ___ tryin' to make His way ___ home? ___

|1. |2., 3.

2. If Tryin' to make His way _____ home, _____

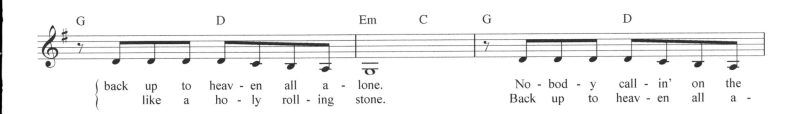

{ back up to heav - en all a - lone.
  like a ho - ly roll - ing stone.

No - bod - y call - in' on the
Back up to heav - en all a -

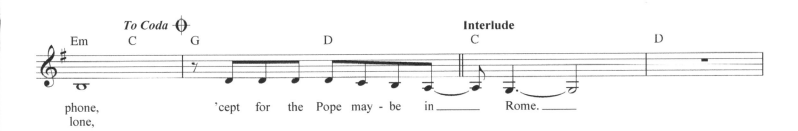

To Coda ⊕ **Interlude**

phone, 'cept for the Pope may - be in ___ Rome. ___
lone,

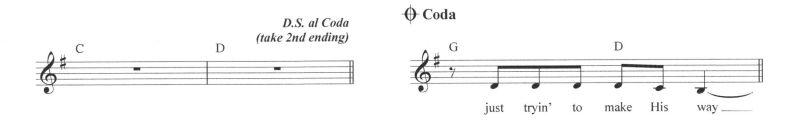

D.S. al Coda
(take 2nd ending)

⊕ **Coda**

just tryin' to make His way ___

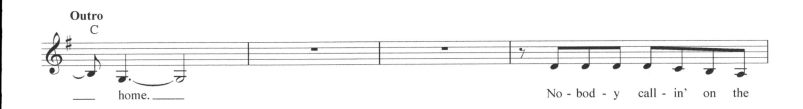

Outro

___ home. ___ No - bod - y call - in' on the

phone, 'cept for the Pope may - be in Rome.

Save Tonight

Words and Music by Eagle Eye Cherry

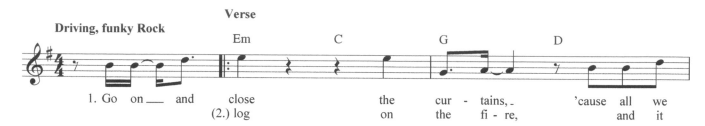

First note

Verse

Driving, funky Rock

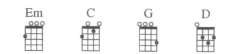

1. Go on ___ and close the cur - tains, ___ 'cause all we
(2.) log on the fi - re, and it

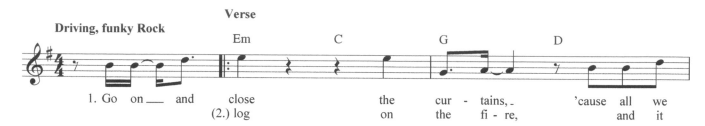

need is can - dle - light. You and ___ me, and a
burns like me ___ for ___ you. To - mor - row comes with

bot - tle of wine, ___ gon - na hold you to - night, ah, yeah. ___ Well, we
one de - si - re, to take me a - way, it's true. ___ It ain't

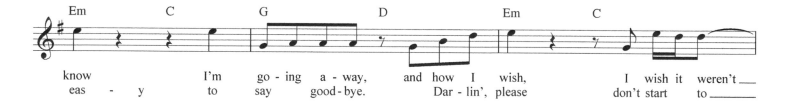

know I'm go - ing a - way, and how I wish, I wish it weren't ___
eas - y to say good - bye. Dar - lin', please don't start to ___

___ so. So take this wine, ___ and drink with me. ___
___ cry. 'Cause, girl, you know I've got to go.

% Chorus

Let's de - lay our mis - er - y.)
Lord, I wish it was - n't so.)   Save to - night, and

fight the break _ of dawn. Come ___ to - mor - row, to - mor - row I'll _ be gone. Save ___

___ to - night, and fight the break _ of dawn. Come ___ to - mor - row, to -

mor - row I'll _ be gone. 2. There's a mor - row I'll _ be gone. To - mor - row comes to

take me a - way. I wish that I, that I could stay.

Girl, you know I've got to go, oh. Lord, I wish it was - n't so.

Save to - mor - row I'll _ be gone. To -

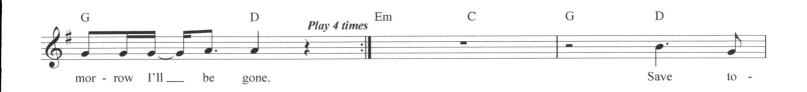

mor - row I'll _ be gone. Save to -

night. Save to - night.

The Scientist

Words and Music by Guy Berryman, Jon Buckland, Will Champion and Chris Martin

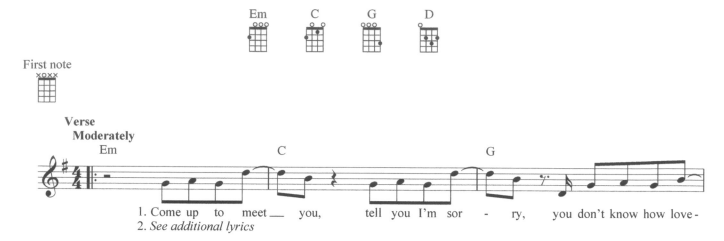

First note

Verse
Moderately

1. Come up to meet _ you, tell you I'm sor - ry, you don't know how love-
2. *See additional lyrics*

- ly you are. ___ I had to find ___ you, tell you I need ___

___ you, tell you I'll set ___ you a - part. ___ Tell me your se -

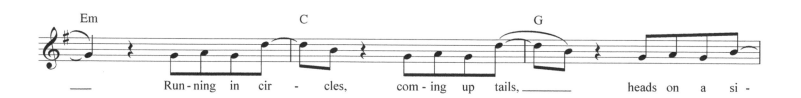

- crets and ask me your ques - tions, oh, let's go back to the start. ___

Run - ning in cir - cles, com - ing up tails, ___ heads on a si -

Chorus

- lence a - part. ___ No - bod - y said ___ it was eas - y. ___

Oh, it's such a shame for us to part. No - bod - y said

it was eas - y. No one ev - er said it would be { this hard. / so hard. }

Oh, take me } back to the start.
I'm go - ing }

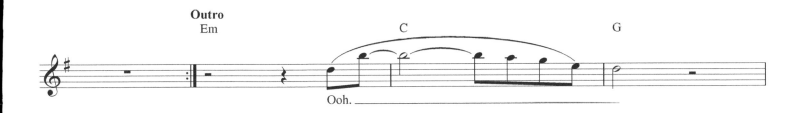

Outro

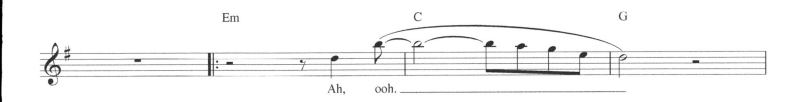

Ooh.

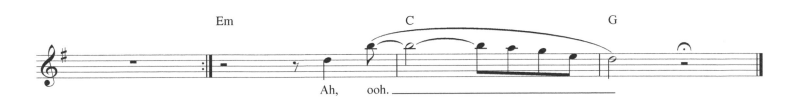

Ah, ooh.

Ah, ooh.

Additional Lyrics

2. I was just guessing at numbers and figures,
   Pulling the puzzles apart.
   Questions of science, science and progress
   Do not speak as loud as my heart.
   And tell me you love me, come back and haunt me.
   Oh, and I rush to the start.
   Running in circles, chasing our tails,
   Coming back as we are.

Slip Slidin' Away

Words and Music by Paul Simon

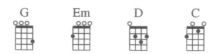

First note

Slip slid - in' a - way. Slip slid - in' a -

way. You know the

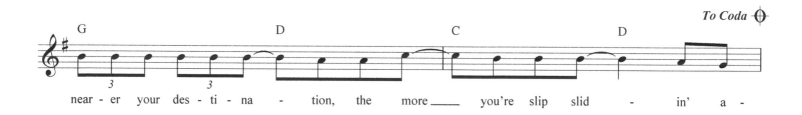

near - er your des - ti - na - tion, the more _____ you're slip slid - in' a -

way. 1. I know a man; _____
2.–4. *See additional lyrics*

he came from my home - town. ___ He wore his

pas - sion ___ for his wom - an like a thorn - y crown. He said, "Do -

lor - es, _____ I _____ live in fear. _____

My love for you's so o - ver - pow'r - ing I'm a - fraid ___

___ that I _____ will dis - ap - pear." Slip slid - in' a -

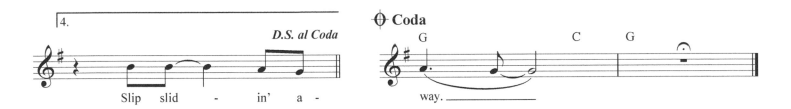

Slip slid - in' a - way. _____

Additional Lyrics

2. And I know a woman; became a wife.
   These are the very words she uses to describe her life.
   She said, "A good day ain't got no rain."
   She said, "A bad day's when I lie in bed and think of things that might have been."

3. And I know a father who had a son.
   He longed to tell him all the reasons for the things he'd done.
   He came a long way just to explain.
   He kissed his boy as he lay sleeping, then he turned around and headed home again.

4. God only knows. God makes His plan.
   The information's unavailable to the mortal man.
   We're workin' our jobs, collect our pay,
   Believe we're glidin' down the highway, when in fact, we're slip slidin' away.

Stand by Me

Words and Music by Jerry Leiber, Mike Stoller and Ben E. King

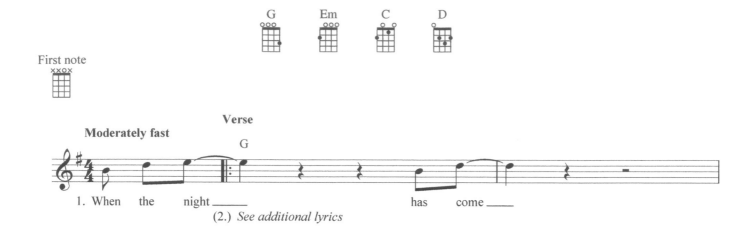

First note

Verse

Moderately fast

1. When the night _____ has come _____

(2.) *See additional lyrics*

and the land is dark, ___ and the moon _____ is the on-

- ly light we'll see, no, I won't ___

_____ be a - fraid, ___ oh, I _____ won't be a -

fraid, just as long _____ as you stand, ___

_____ stand by _____ me. So, dar - lin', dar - lin',

Chorus

stand _____ by me, _____ oh, _____ stand _____ by _____

me. Oh, stand, — stand by _____ me,

stand by _____ me. 2. If the sky — Dar - lin', dar - lin',

Outro-Chorus

stand _____ by me, _____ oh, _____ stand _____

— by _____ me. Oh, stand, —

stand by _____ me, stand by _____ me.

Additional Lyrics

2. If the sky that we look upon should tumble and fall,
   Or the mountains should crumble to the sea,
   I won't cry, I won't cry. No, I won't shed a tear,
   Just as long as you stand, stand by me.
   And darlin', darlin'... (*To Chorus*)

The Story

Words and Music by Phil Hanseroth

Additional Lyrics

2. I climbed across the mountaintops,
   Swam all across the ocean blue.
   I crossed all the lines and I broke all the rules,
   But, baby, I broke them all for you.
   Oh, because even when I was flat broke,
   You made me feel like a million bucks. You do.
   I was made for you.

3. You see the smile that's on my mouth?
   It's hiding the words that don't come out.
   All of my friends who think that I'm blessed,
   They don't know my head is a mess.
   No, they don't know who I really am,
   And they don't know what I've been through like you do.
   And I was made for you.

Push

Written by Rob Thomas with Matt Serletic

First note

Moderate Rock

Verse

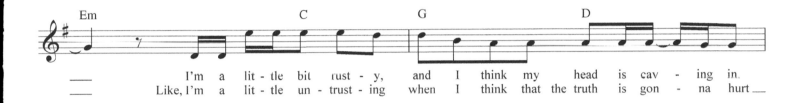

1. She said, "I don't know if I've ev-er been good e-nough. ___
(2.) "I don't know why you ev-er would lie to me." ___

___ I'm a lit-tle bit rust-y, and I think my head is cav-ing in.
Like, I'm a lit-tle un-trust-ing when I think that the truth is gon-na hurt ___

___ ya. I don't know if I've ev-er been real-ly loved ___
And I don't know why you could-n't just stay ___ with ___

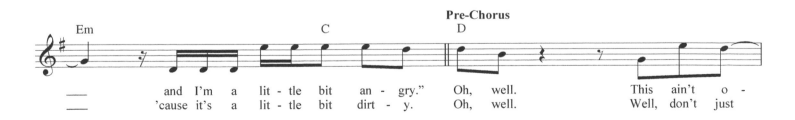

___ by a hand that's touched me. And I feel like some-thing's goin' to give, ___
___ me. You could-n't stand to be near me when my face don't seem to wan-na shine ___

Pre-Chorus

___ and I'm a lit-tle bit an-gry." Oh, well. This ain't o-
___ 'cause it's a lit-tle bit dirt-y. Oh, well. Well, don't just

-ver,   no, not here.   Not while I still need you a - round.___
stand there,   say nice things ___ to me   'cause I've been cheat- ed, I've been wronged. And

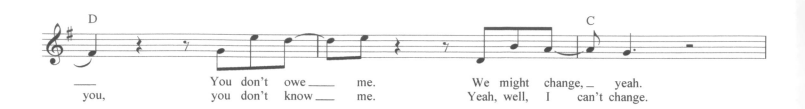

___   You don't owe ___ me.   We might change, ___ yeah.
you,   you don't know ___ me.   Yeah, well, I can't change.

%S Chorus

Yeah, we just might feel   good.   I wan - na push you a - round.
Well, I won't do an - y - thing at all.

Well, I will,   well, I will.   I wan - na push you ___ down.   Well, I will,   well, I will.

To Coda ⊕

I wan - na take you for grant - ed.   I wan - na take you for grant-

ed, yeah, yeah, I will and I will,___   and I ___

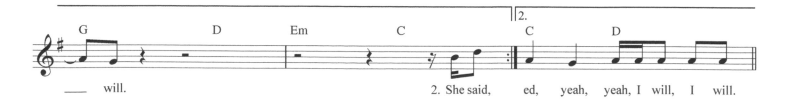

___ will.   2. She said, ed, yeah, yeah, I will, I will.

Bridge

Oh, but don't bowl me o - ver. Just wait a min - ute, well, it kind-a fell a -

part. Things get so cra - zy, cra - zy. Don't rush this, ba -

D.S. al Coda

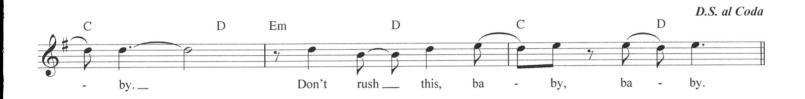

- by. Don't rush this, ba - by, ba - by.

Coda

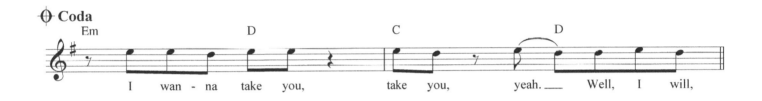

I wan - na take you, take you, yeah. Well, I will,

Outro

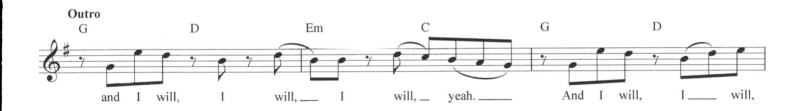

and I will, I will, I will, yeah. And I will, I will,

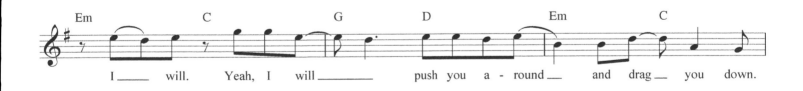

I will. Yeah, I will push you a - round and drag you down.

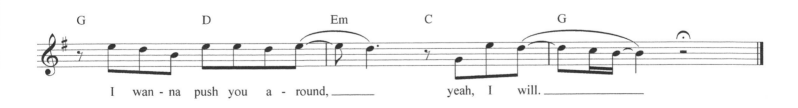

I wan - na push you a - round, yeah, I will.

The Swimming Song

Words and Music by Loudon Wainwright III

Additional Lyrics

2. This summer I did the backstroke, and you know that that's not all.
I did the breaststroke and the butterfly and the old Australian crawl,
The old Australian crawl.
This summer I swam in a public place and a reservoir to boot.
At the latter I was informal, at the former I wore my suit,
I wore my swimming suit.

3. This summer I did swan dives and jackknives for you all.
But once, when you weren't looking, I did a cannonball,
Did a cannonball.
This summer I went swimming. This summer I might have drowned.
But I held my breath and I kicked my feet and I moved my arms around,
Moved my arms around.

A Teenager in Love

Words by Doc Pomus
Music by Mort Shuman

Additional Lyrics

2. One day I feel so happy, next day I feel so sad.
   I guess I'll learn to take the good with the bad.

3. If you want to make me cry, that won't be so hard to do.
   And if you should say goodbye, I'll still go on loving you.

This One's for the Girls

Words and Music by Aimee Mayo, Hillary Lindsey and Chris Lindsey

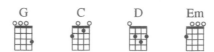

First note

Verse
Moderately

1. This is for all ___ you girls ___ a-bout ___ thir-teen. ___
2., 3. *See additional lyrics*

High school can be ___ so rough, ___ can be ___ so mean. ___ Hold ___ on ___

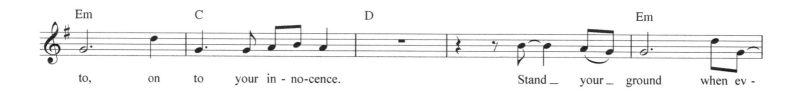

to, on to your in-no-cence. Stand ___ your ___ ground when ev-

- 'ry-bod-y's giv-in' in. This ___ one's for the girls. ___ one's for the girls ___

Chorus

___ who've ev-er had a bro-ken heart, ___ who've wished ___

___ up - on a shoot - ing star. ___ You're beau - ti - ful the way you are. ___ This ___

___ one's for the girls ___ who love ___ with-out hold-ing back, ___ who dream ___

___ with ev - 'ry-thing they have, ___ all a - round ___ the world. This ___

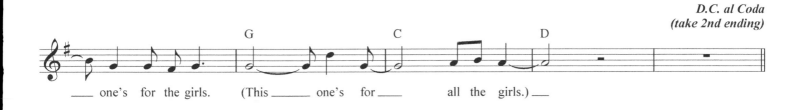

___ one's for the girls. (This ___ one's for ___ all the girls.) ___

Coda

___ one's for the girls. Yeah, ___ we're all ___ the same ___ in - side ___ (the same ___

___ in - side), ___ from one ___ to nine-ty - nine. ___ This ___ one's for the girls ___

Chorus

who've ev - er had a bro-ken heart, _____ who've wished _ up-on a shoot - ing star. _

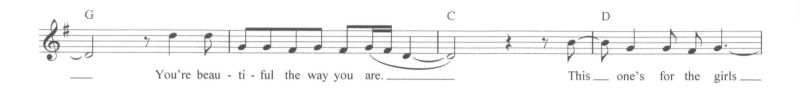

_ You're beau - ti - ful the way you are. _____ This __ one's for the girls __

who love __ with-out hold-ing back, _____ who dream _ with ev -'ry-thing they have, _

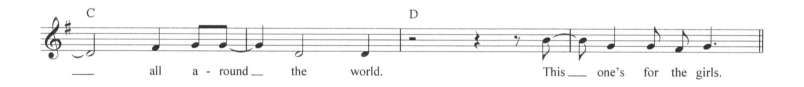

_ all a - round __ the world. This __ one's for the girls.

Outro

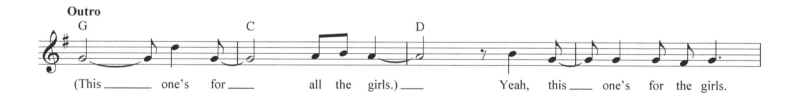

(This _____ one's for _____ all the girls.) __ Yeah, this __ one's for the girls.

(This _____ one's for _____ all the girls.) __

Additional Lyrics

2. This is for all you girls about twenty-five
In little apartments, just tryin' to get by,
Livin' on, on dreams and Spaghetti-O's,
Wonderin' where your life's gonna go.

3. This is for all you girls about forty-two,
Tossin' pennies in the fountain of youth.
Every laugh, laugh line on your face
Made you who you are today.

Today Was a Fairytale

Words and Music by Taylor Swift

First note

Verse
Moderately, in 2

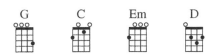

1. To - day was a fair - y - tale. You were the prince. I used to be a
3. *See additional lyrics*

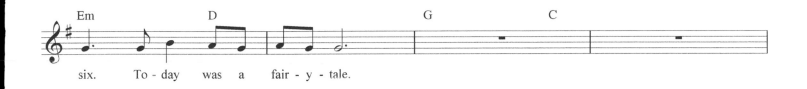

dam - sel in dis - tress. You took me by the hand and you picked me up at

six. To - day was a fair - y - tale.

Verse

2. To - day was a fair - y - tale. I wore a
4. *See additional lyrics*

dress, you wore a dark grey T - shirt. You told me I was

pret - ty when I looked like a mess. To - day was a fair - y - tale.

Pre-Chorus

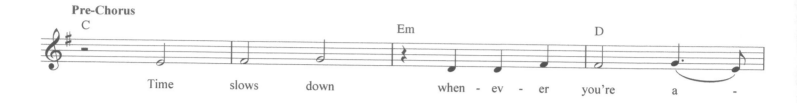

Time slows down when - ev - er you're a -

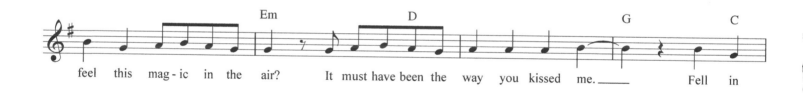

round. _____ But can you

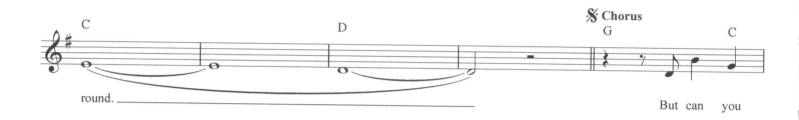

feel this mag - ic in the air? It must have been the way you kissed me. ____ Fell in

love when I saw you stand - in' there. It must -'ve been the way to - day was a

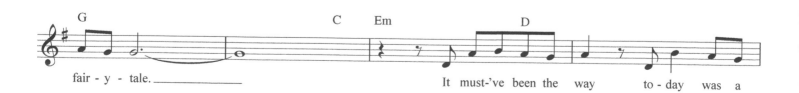

fair - y - tale. _____ It must -'ve been the way to - day was a

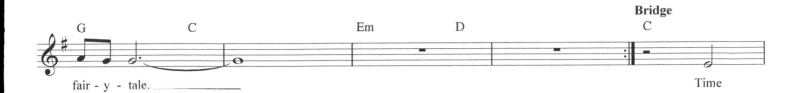

fair - y - tale. _____

Time

slows   down   when - ev - er   you're   a - round.   I   can

feel   my   heart;   it's   beat - ing   in ___ my   chest. ___   Did   you

feel   it?   I   can't   put   this   down. _____

D.S. al Coda

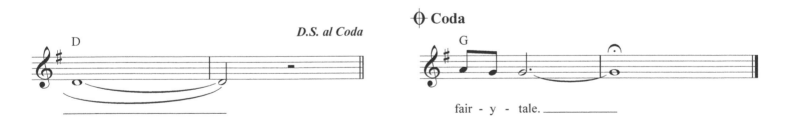

Coda

fair - y - tale. _____

Additional Lyrics

3. Today was a fairytale.
   You've got a smile
   Takes me to another planet.
   Every move you make,
   Everything you say is right.
   Today was a fairytale.

4. Today was a fairytale.
   All that I can say
   Is now it's getting so much clearer.
   Nothing made sense
   Till the time I saw your face.
   Today was a fairytale.

3 AM

Lyrics by Rob Thomas
Music by Rob Thomas, Brian Yale, John Leslie Goff and John Joseph Stanley

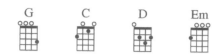

First note

Intro
Moderately fast

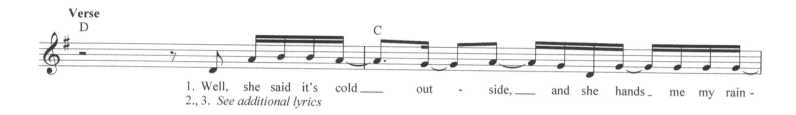

Verse

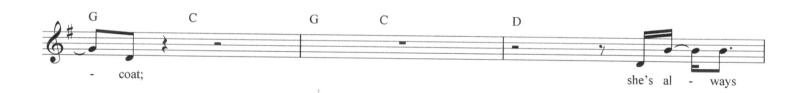

1. Well, she said it's cold ___ out - side, ___ and she hands ___ me my rain -

2., 3. *See additional lyrics*

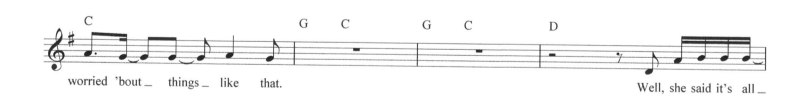

- coat;   she's al - ways

worried 'bout ___ things ___ like   that.   Well, she said it's all ___

___ gon - na end ___ and it might as well ___ be my ___ fault.

Pre-Chorus

And she on - ly sleeps when it's rain - ing, and she screams

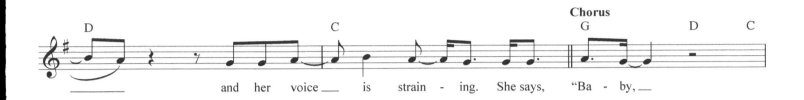

and her voice is strain - ing. She says, "Ba - by,

Chorus

it's three A. M. I must be lone - ly." When she says,

"Ba - by," well, I can't help but be scared of it all

some - times. And the rain's gon - na wash a - way; I be - lieve it.

1.

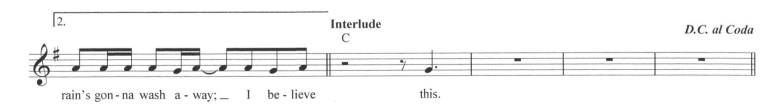

2.

Interlude

D.C. al Coda

rain's gon - na wash a - way; I be - lieve this.

But out - side it's stopped rain - ing, _____ yeah. But she _ says,

Outro-Chorus

"Ba - by, _____   well, it's three A. M. _ I must _ be lone -
this. _____   Well, it's three A. M. _ I must _ be lone -

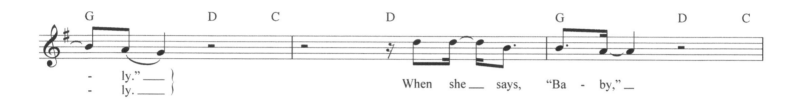

- ly." _ }   When she _ says, "Ba - by," _
- ly. _ }

well, I can't help _ but be scared _ of it all _____ some - times. And the

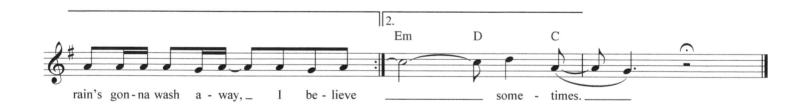

rain's gon-na wash a - way, _ I be - lieve _____ some - times. _____

Additional Lyrics

2. Well, she's got a little bit of something;
   God, it's better than nothing.
   And in her color portrait world,
   She believes that she's got it all.
   She swears the moon don't hang
   Quite as high as it used to.

3. Well, she believes that life isn't made up
   Of all that she's used to.
   And the clock on the wall has been stuck
   At three for days and days.
   She thinks that happiness
   Is a mat that sits on her doorway.

With or Without You

Words and Music by U2

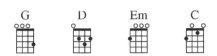

First note

Intro
Moderately

See the stone ___ set in your eyes, ___ see the thorn ___ ___ twist in your side. ___ I'll wait ___ for you. ___

Verse

1. Sleight of hand ___ and twist of fate, ___ on a bed of nails ___ ___ she makes me wait, ___ and I wait ___ with - out ___ you, ___
2. Through the storm ___ we reach the shore. ___ You give it all, ___ ___ but I want more, ___ and I'm wait - ing for ___ you, ___

Chorus

with or with-out ___ you, ___ with or with - out ___ you.
with or with-out ___ you, ___

2. D ... Em ... C ... G
with or with - out you, __ uh - huh. __ I can't live __

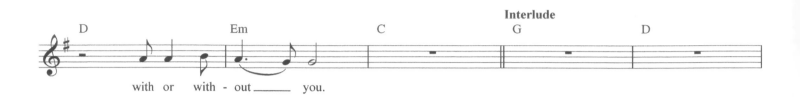

D ... Em ... C ... G ... D
Interlude
with or with - out __ you.

Em ... C ... 𝄋 **Bridge** G ... D
And you give your-self a - way. __ And you give __

Em ... C ... G
__ your - self a - way. __ And you give, __ and you give, __

D ... Em ... **To Coda** ⊕ C
__ and you give your - self a - way. __

Verse
G ... D ... Em
3. My hands are tied, __ my bod - y bruised. __

C ... G ... D
__ You got __ me with __ noth - ing to win __ and __

noth - ing left ___ to lose. ___ And you _____ With or with - out ___

Chorus

___ you, ___ with or with - out you, ___ oh. _____ I can't live ___

Interlude

___ with or with - out _____ you. ___ Oh. _____

___ Oh. _____ Oh, _____ oh, oh. ___

Outro-Chorus

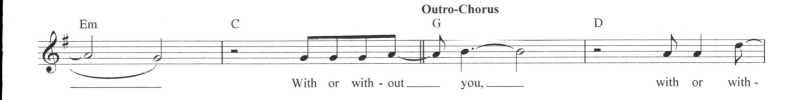

_____ With or with - out _____ you, _____ with or with -

- out you, ___ uh - huh. ___ I can't live ___ with or with -

out _____ you, with or with - out you. ___

Two Princes

Words and Music by Spin Doctors

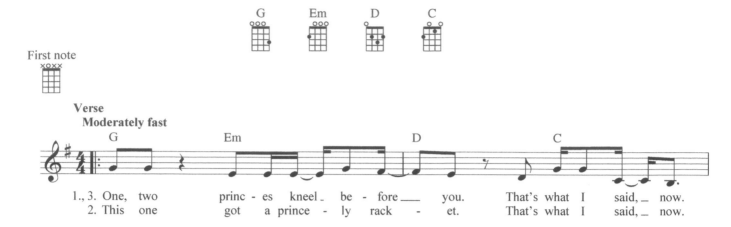

First note

Verse
Moderately fast

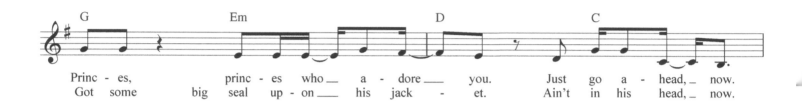

1., 3. One, two princ - es kneel __ be - fore __ you. That's what I said, __ now.
2. This one got a prince - ly rack - et. That's what I said, __ now.

Princ - es, princ - es who a - dore __ you. Just go a - head, __ now.
Got some big seal up - on __ his jack - et. Ain't in his head, __ now.

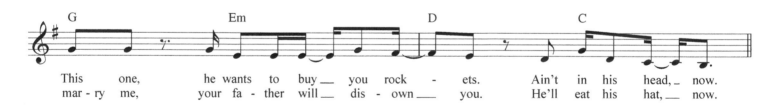

One has dia - monds in __ his pock - ets. That's some bread, __ now.
Mar - ry him, your fa - ther will __ con - done __ you. How 'bout that, __ now? You

This one, he wants to buy __ you rock - ets. Ain't in his head, __ now.
mar - ry me, your fa - ther will __ dis - own __ you. He'll eat his hat, __ now.

1.

Interlude

Yeah, _____ yeah, yeah. ___ (Di di ba dip. Di dip dip di dip. Ba dee - dle - ee

di ba du ba du ba du ba du ba du ba du ba du ba.)

Pre-Chorus

Mar - ry him or mar - ry me. I'm ___ the one that loves you, ba - by. Can't you see? I ain't

got no fu - ture or a fam - 'ly tree, _ but I know what a prince and lov - er ought to be. ___

I know what a prince and lov - er ought to be. ___ Said, if you want to call ___ me, ba -

- by, just go a - head, _ now. And if you'd like to tell ___ me may -

- be, just go a - head, _ now. And if you wan - na buy ___ me flow -

- ers, just go a - head, _ now. And if you'd like to talk ___ for ho -

- urs, just go a - head, _ now.   - urs, just go a - head, _ now.

Wagon Wheel

Words and Music by Bob Dylan and Ketch Secor

First note

Verse
Moderately fast Country (♩♩ = ♩♪)

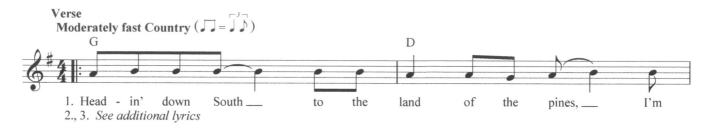

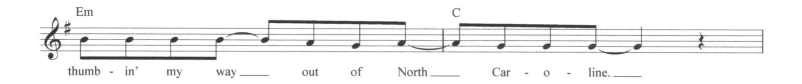

1. Head - in' down South ___ to the land of the pines, ___ I'm
2., 3. *See additional lyrics*

thumb - in' my way ___ out of North ___ Car - o - line.

Starin' up the road ___ and pray to God I ___ see head -

- lights.   I made it down the coast in

sev - en - teen hours. ___ Pick - in' me a bou - quet of dog -

- wood flow'rs. ___ And I'm a - hop - in' for Ra - leigh, I can

see my ba - by to-night. _____ So, rock ___ me, ma - ma, like a

wag - on wheel. _ Rock ___ me, ma - ma, an - y way you feel. __ Hey, _

_____ ma - ma, rock ___ me. Rock _

___ me, ma - ma, like the wind and the rain. __ Rock ___ me, ma - ma, like a

To Coda ⊕

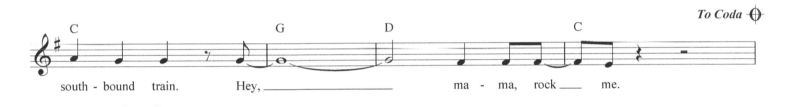

south - bound train. Hey, _____ ma - ma, rock ___ me.

D.S. al Coda   ⊕ **Coda**

Oh, _____ so rock _

Additional Lyrics

2. Runnin' from the cold up in New England,
   I was born to be a fiddler in an old-time string band.
   My baby plays the guitar, I pick a banjo now.
   Oh, North Country winters keep a-gettin' me down.
   Lost my money playin' poker, so I had to leave town.
   But I ain't turnin' back to livin' that old life no more.

3. Walkin' through the South out of Roanoke,
   I caught a trucker out of Philly, had a nice long toke.
   But he's a-headin' west from the Cumberland Gap to Johnson City, Tennessee.
   I got, I gotta move on before the sun.
   I hear my baby callin' my name and I know that she's the only one.
   And if I die in Raleigh, at least I will die free.

Wonderful Tonight

Words and Music by Eric Clapton

First note

Bridge

I feel won - der - ful ____ be - cause I see ____ the love ____

____ light in ____ your eyes. Then the won - der of it all ____ is that you

just don't re - al - ize ____ how much ____ I love ____ you." *(Instrumental)*

D.C. al Coda   **Coda**

Outro

Oh, my dar - ling, you are won - der - ful ____ to - night." ____

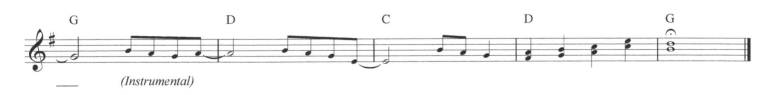

____ *(Instrumental)*

Zombie

Lyrics and Music by Dolores O'Riordan

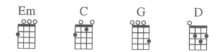

First note

Verse
Heavy Rock beat

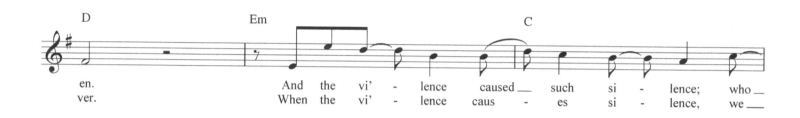

1. An - oth - er head ___ hangs low - ly, child ___ is slow - ly tak -
2. An - oth - er moth - er's break - ing heart ___ is tak - ing o -

en. And the vi' - lence caused ___ such si - lence; who ___
ver. When the vi' - lence caus - es si - lence, we ___

_____ are we ___ mis - tak - en? But, you see, it's not me, it's not my
_____ must be ___ mis - tak - en. It's the same old ___ theme since ___ nine -

Pre-Chorus

fam - i - ly. In your head, ___ in your head they are fight - ing _____ with their tanks
- teen six - teen. In your head, ___ in your head they're still fight - ing _____ with their tanks

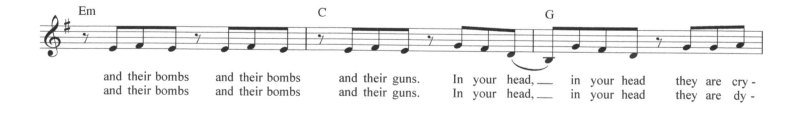

and their bombs and their bombs and their guns. In your head, ___ in your head they are cry -
and their bombs and their bombs and their guns. In your head, ___ in your head they are dy -

ing, _____ } in your head, _____ in your head, _____ zom - bie,
ing, _____ }

zom - bie, zom - bie, hey, __ hey. __ What's in your head, _____ in your

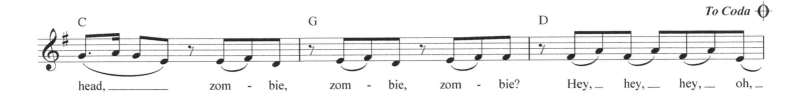

head, _____ zom - bie, zom - bie, zom - bie? Hey, __ hey, __ hey, __ oh, __

__ do, do, do, do, do, do, do, do, do, do, do, do,

do, do, do, do. _____

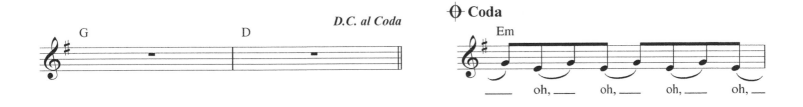

__ oh, ___ oh, __ oh, __ oh, __

__ oh, ___ oh, __ hey, __ oh, _____ ya, ya. _____

Who'll Stop the Rain

Words and Music by John Fogerty

1. Long as I___ re-mem-ber, the rain___ been com-in' down.___
2., 3. *See additional lyrics*

Clouds of mys-t'ry pour-in' con-fu-sion on___ the ground.___

Good men through___ the ag-es tryin' to find the sun;___

and I won-der, still I won-der, who'll stop the rain?___

Additional Lyrics

2. I went down Virginia, seekin' shelter from the storm.
Caught up in the fable, I watched the tower grow.
Five-year plans and new deals wrapped in golden chains;
And I wonder, still I wonder, who'll stop the rain?

3. Heard the singers playin'; how we cheered for more.
The crowd had rushed together, tryin' to keep warm.
Still the rain kept pourin', fallin' on my ears;
And I wonder, still I wonder, who'll stop the rain?